Thrive
WELL

A SIMPLE GUIDE TO
AVOID BURNOUT AND MAXIMISE
YOUR FULL POTENTIAL

DEBORAH HULME

Dedicated to

My Father – Stuart Hulme
The man who made me who I am

Foreword

*I*f you are looking to up-level your life, to thrive amid a relentlessly changing, demanding world. If you want to be well, stay well and perform well personally and professionally. If you are curious to learn and grow in Mind, Body, and Spirit. If you are looking for that something, that piece of magic that might just shift the needle in your life, enhancing your capacity to expand and grow, then where do you go and who do you go to?

You go to someone who has not only done it, but has done even more. You go to someone who has a track record. You go to someone who is totally dedicated to mastering life and helping others do the same. You go to someone who is not afraid to tell you the truth and get into the nitty-gritty of life. You go to someone who is totally dedicated to sharing the wisdom she has gained.

Deborah Hulme is one such woman. She is a remarkable, highly intelligent, and deeply feeling woman. She is a brilliant teacher, communicator, life-affirming human being, and a successful entrepreneur to boot. Her track record is phenomenal.

How do I know? How can I write this and stand by it? Because I have worked very closely with Deborah. Together we have navigated some of the most challenging of situations. I know her mettle. I know her dedication. I know her resilience. Above all, I know her honesty, integrity, and authenticity – her deep humanity. I know that she is living proof of this book. Deborah is the real deal. What she shares in *Thrive Well* is wonderful, timeless, practical, and meaningful material that cannot help but contribute to any reader's journey.

Life can be tough – sometimes very, very tough. Navigating our business and personal lives; managing our emotions; our mental, physical, spiritual, social, financial challenges, and more: every day of our lives can be hugely taxing. It requires energy, focus, and strategic and behavioural skills to live with any sort of equanimity, let alone to thrive and grow personally and professionally.

Deborah's book delivers tools, practical exercises, and insights that work. They are accessible and comprehensible. I recommend it wholeheartedly. These are the words of a continual learner on becoming the very best version of herself, sharing her practical, effective, and proven wisdom and strategies along the way. You will not regret making friends with this book. When you do, not only will you want to share it, but you will also be able to savour the magic of the woman who wrote it.

Dr Kim A. Jobst MA. DM. FRCP. MFHom.
Consultant Physician
Functional Shift Consulting Ltd.
London, UK

Preface - Singin' in the Rain

L ife is certainly a journey. What kind of journey we make it is down to us.

My life journey began in a cowshed, singing my heart out early each morning surrounded by cow dung and the grey concrete walls of the shed, positioned just behind the dairy. My family were farmers. Not poor and not rich. We made our living milking cows and selling milk. For me, growing up meant early mornings before school; a life surrounded by fields and animals rather than concrete and humans, which I am more used to now, living as I do in the sprawling metropolises of London and Milan.

I remember it as a simple life: hard, yet straightforward in its own way. But what I remember most, as I approach my sixth decade and look back over my life, is me as a 14-year-old girl, dressed in a blue boiler suit and green wellies, singing away as I shovelled the cow dung out of the milking parlour and into the slurry tanks outside. My favourite song was *Singin' in the Rain*. The scraper had a long handle and a large wide rubber end – ideal for scraping dung from a concrete floor. More importantly, it could also double as a make-believe microphone, allowing me to belt out songs at full volume while I twizzled and tap-danced over the rubber end in a style that was more than a match for Gene Kelly.

OK, maybe I was not always in tune, which is probably why my long-suffering father used to occasionally put his head through the window, yelling at me to pipe down as I was scaring the men, the horses, and shredding his nerves. I did not care. I was happy. Really happy. As I danced around that dung shovel, my heart felt like it would burst with all the hopes and dreams for my future. I knew I would never be a singer or a dancer, but I knew I would be something. The potential and opportunity that surrounded me in that shed every morning was an energy source that lifted me up to the sky, and I loved it.

And now, today, I am something. I am me. It did not just happen though. It was not that easy. My life was no musical: there was no Gene Kelly to lead me effortlessly through the dance of life, and certainly no one had taught me the moves beforehand. It has been a long and, at times, tortuous journey filled with many lessons, setbacks, failures, and falls along the way.

But I am here now: still standing, still smiling, and still singing badly. Getting here has been a process of learning, unlearning, and relearning, as I worked to understand the human system, the neuroscience behind how the brain works, and what we need to really thrive when going through the challenges and setbacks of life.

As I have grown, life has shown and taught me many lessons. The most significant is that happiness, the ability to be truly free in the moment, to find joy in the smallest of things, can happen spontaneously. More often than not, though, it has to be deliberately sustained – a choice, which, at times, feels seemingly impossible, but it is a choice all the same. A choice that, importantly, we can all make.

Most of the time, we don't think about happiness or even our sense of general wellbeing as a choice. Instead, we live life as a series of peaks and troughs, with the ups and downs every so often overwhelming, feeling more like an emotional roller coaster than a 'steady as you go' sailing experience. It certainly did for me.

When I was dancing in the dung as a young teenager, I was naturally happy and well. It was a sensation specifically tied to what was happening to me in that moment. I did not know how to sustain the feeling, and I did not know how to repeatedly generate the feeling at will. Being in a state of happiness was either there or not there, and it could disappear like the wind, dependent on my energy levels, thoughts, external events, or people saying and doing things to 'upset' me.

As life progressed, I noticed that, unlike myself, there were people who did somehow manage to maintain a balanced, happy state – to stay well and perform well, even when things were not always going their way. They were more resilient, able to flow through life relatively smoothly, adapting and flexing, with seemingly little effort. There was no correlation I could easily identify that linked these people together: not money, status, career choice, ages, or backgrounds. But exist they did, and it piqued my curiosity. I wanted to know how they did it, what made them distinct from me, and how could I be more like them.

And so my learning journey began. I studied the habits and behaviours of such individuals; I read, learned, observed, and practised many different frameworks, models, and techniques, all of which proclaimed to build resilience and support personal change. Some were brilliant, others not so much.

I have coached and been coached on my journey; I have learned the importance of looking after the self and the art of gratitude and forgiveness; I have learned how to manage my emotions rather than be ruled by them; I have learned how to tame my own thoughts and how to stop the incessant noise inside my own head, terrorising me every day. In short, I have learned how to care for myself, how to love myself, and how to find my happy place.

It is fair to say I am still a work-in-progress. I still have my down moments, and I probably will until my last breath. I can say, however, with absolute certainty, that the difference to my life has been transformational in my relationships with my family, friends, and work groups.

Most of us spend large chunks of our lives doubting our capability and beating ourselves up for not being enough, for being unable to cope as well as those around us. My own life changed dramatically the day I woke up and realised that the only person holding me back, the only person who was sapping my resilience and happiness, was me – led by my own fear of failure, my own lack of courage, and my own inability to change.

It is easy to blame external events, people, and circumstances for what happens to us. However, it keeps us stuck. It takes away the necessity for us to act, to do something. I would never get in a car, take the wheel, but then give control of the gears over to someone else before driving off. So why was I allowing external events to drive my life? And, more importantly, why allow external events to drive yours?

I hope you enjoy these pages. I have aimed to share with you the best of my learnings from the sciences as well as business and life experiences, introducing you to new ways of thinking and caring about you, all of which contribute to a happier, more balanced life. Your journey will be different from mine. Some of my learnings will resonate and some will not. Either way, I hope you enjoy them and that you find your experience to be just as freeing. I also hope you will write and tell me about it! I'd love to know how you are getting on ☺.

Table of Contents

Introduction

This book brings together a mix of skills and understanding gained from working across a spectrum of national and international businesses. It's a combination of my neuroscience, communication, engagement, and change expertise, including the discoveries I've made from working with leaders and managers with the goal to evolve and broaden leadership practice.

I have been tremendously fortunate to work alongside many amazing individuals who have challenged me to continually grow, expand, and learn. In addition, where relevant, I've included references to additional information sources and reading materials that I've personally found helpful along the way.

During the latter part of my career, the learnings from the behavioural sciences and particularly those flowing from the field of neuroscience caught my attention and changed how I lived my life. It is this knowledge that I most want to share with you, and my wish is that you find the content captured in the following parts as life-changing as I did.

To be honest, understanding more about how we function as human beings saved me. I've had my own setbacks and emotional knocks and certainly spent a great deal of my 30s believing that I was not worthy, that I would never be seen as a 'good' person – whatever a good person is. I found it easier to look for love outside of myself than to actually love myself.

How was it possible for me to love myself when I was clearly such a troublesome person? I believed this to be true and had been told so, many times over. Of course, this lack of care for the self led to many unfortunate consequences and had become the ultimate culmination of many beliefs seeded during childhood.

Thankfully, I stumbled upon the science behind how the brain works. I learned that we are simply a reflection of what we put out, that the brain changes throughout our lifetime, that we do not have to stay stuck in unhelpful patterns of thinking and behaving. Even more importantly, I realised I already had all the resources I needed within me to completely change how I viewed myself and, consequently, the trajectory of my life.

When the penny finally dropped that what I put out is what comes back and, even more importantly, that I can proactively manage what I put out, everything changed. I knew that if I became intentional about who I wanted to be and started to develop more productive habits, I could reshape myself. Integral to this, though, and perhaps the hardest part of all, was learning to love myself.

And so began a slow and sometimes arduous journey that is still going on to this day. The first time I looked at me in the mirror and told me that I loved myself, that I was proud of myself, I cried. It was painful and difficult. It's not easy shifting baked-in beliefs that have been with you for many years.

Interestingly, the most wonderful thing I discovered was that the more I loved myself, the more love came back to me, and the more life blossomed. Roll forward a couple of decades and I am a totally different person. I broke myself apart to put myself back together again. Was it easy? No. Is it really that powerful? Yes. If you're looking for a quick fix, I'm afraid you are in the wrong place. However, if you want to understand the steps that will take you towards a different way of living and thinking about yourself, then you are exactly where you need to be.

For any change to manifest in life, the learning must be lived in practice, day-to-day. It takes a certain amount of courage, reflection, and adjustment to embrace such a challenge. It can be a struggle. Still, over time, it becomes easier to see just how far we have come and what a difference the learning has made, both in terms of how we think about ourselves and the ease with which our life flows.

After all, shouldn't we be living the good life compared to previous generations? Instead, many of us are battling a deep sense of overwhelm. Why? Why now? Quite simply, because the human system can't evolve fast enough. The world is changing at an unprecedented rate thanks to technological advancements, the rise of artificial intelligence, changing social norms and values, and much more. As a result, we humans have struggled to keep up. The sheer amount of change we experience, the ongoing distractions we must navigate, and the daily firehose of information we must consume puts enormous strain on an already stretched system.

Does this mean we can't handle it? No, absolutely not. The resources exist within us, but unlike previous generations, our system needs a greater level of care and attention to access and activate those resources. Whereas before we might have got away with poor nutrition, paying little or zero attention to our thoughts, or skipping rest and recovery time, now we can't. Quite simply, to flourish, thrive, and perform, we need to be balanced and healthy.

Thrive Well takes us on that journey with easy-to-follow steps, practical tools, and techniques that can be applied day-to-day. This book is made up of six parts: Self-Care, Brain, Mind, Body, Stress Management, and Social Connection. The parts themselves can be digested in any order. You don't have to read the book from cover to cover; you can choose where to start, moving around the topics to suit your situation. My only guidance is that I highly recommend you begin with Self-Care as this part highlights the need to look after the self, and it guides you to identify which of the other areas may be out of balance and, therefore, where to first focus your attention.

Following is a quick summary of each part to help you navigate your journey through this book.

1: Self-Care

Self-Care is exactly what it says on the tin: an opportunity for you to take a moment to reflect on how well you care for yourself and where you might like to begin your self-awareness journey. It's here to help you identify where to focus your attention and to keep track of how far you have progressed over time. This is particularly helpful when we hit those inevitable walls of frustration, tiredness, or disappointment along the way.

You will find a simple and straightforward assessment questionnaire (Stay Well Assessment), which is designed to guide the start of your learning. In addition, there is space for quiet reflection as you assess your internal energy level, along with your capacity for and comfort with moments of self-compassion. As a side note, you may find it helpful to return to the Stay Well Assessment in Self-Care from time to time, checking your progress to plan as you reflect on any noticeable shifts and changes in the scoring pattern.

2: Brain

In this part, you will learn all you need to know about how to keep the brain fit and healthy. The physical health and structure of the brain is not something we think about much on a daily basis, yet everything we do starts with a chemical reaction in the brain. If the brain is unhealthy, we are unhealthy – no matter how many times we go to the gym or eat our vegetables. Brain health is fundamental to our overall sense of wellbeing, including our physical health.

The brain enables us to grow and learn throughout life; it keeps all the functions that are necessary for survival working. Without it, we would not exist. It might be locked inside our skull; however, there's a lot we can do to support great brain performance, including sleep, nutritious food, and ongoing stimulation. Luckily, we don't need to be neuroscientists to maintain brain health; we just need to be equipped with some basic knowledge.

3: Mind

The part on Mind brings to life the power of thought, introducing practices and frameworks to support more productive thinking patterns. The mind is so powerful. Our thoughts direct our feelings, emotions, behaviours, and, ultimately, our experience of the world. We can think ourselves happy or sad, tired or energised, changing nothing except our thoughts. Of all the things I've learned, the power of the mind is something I wish I had understood from childhood. I wish they taught it in our schools. It makes all the difference to who we are and what we do.

The English poet and intellectual John Milton understood this as far back as 1674 when he wrote his epic poem *Paradise*

Lost, "The mind is its own place, and in itself can make a Heav'n of Hell, a Hell of Heav'n." If we jump forward to the present day, where advances in technology and science have made it possible to understand how the mind changes the brain and the brain influences the mind, we can appreciate and admire just how far-sighted Milton was.

4: Body

In Body, we begin to learn and understand more about the importance of the brain, mind, body connection. The body is intimately connected to the brain and, as such, is constantly relaying messages about our state of wellbeing. This includes signalling when we need to stop, rest, or make changes to our daily activity. If we choose not to listen or we are going at such a pace that we don't hear what it's trying to tell us, the body will eventually shut us down, leaving us with no option other than to collapse into bed and rest.

The body is the container through which we experience the world. The more we understand its functionality and why it responds in the way it does, the more we can improve our overall health and sense of wellbeing. Good nutrition, sleep, and exercise are all important; however, there are additional ways we can create a happy body experience – by understanding the nervous system and the tools we have available to activate (power up) or deactivate (calm) it.

5: Stress Management

During Stress Management, we learn about the importance of cultivating a positive stress mindset, and we'll explore tools and techniques we can use every day to support proactive stress management for reduced anxiety and higher performance. Stress is often positioned as the enemy of a healthy human system and something to always be avoided. Yet, the stress response is a natural component of who we are. If it did not exist, we would not be able to get out of bed in the mornings. When stress is managed well, it actually supports performance and ensures we are on point for those hard-to-do meetings or tasks.

Difficulty arises when we over activate the nervous system and flip it into a state of ongoing chronic stress. Therefore, what we really want to avoid is chronic stress, and that becomes easier to do when we understand how and why the stress response functions the way it does. If we know our stress threshold, can recognise our stress triggers, and have a programme of activity we can call on to deactivate the stress response when needed, it is certain to become a helpful part of our lives.

6: Social Connection

In Social Connection, we explore just how necessary good relationships and connection with others are to our happiness and stability. We often consider social pain to be a poor relation to physical pain, yet, as we'll learn, the opposite is true.

We are social animals, and when we become disconnected or experience various forms of isolation, we suffer. Worse, isolation is insidious, creeping up on us quietly and slowly so that we hardly notice – that is, until the days arrive where we are constantly tired and lethargic for no reason and don't even feel like stepping out of the front door.

The lonelier we become, the less we want to socialise, even though that is exactly what is required to break the downward spiral towards loneliness and, ultimately, depression. Social Connection explains why we should never underestimate the need for relationships and belonging regardless of whether we are introvert or extrovert. In addition, Social Connection highlights the link with happiness and what we can do to create more opportunities for connection.

In Summary

The knowledge, tools, and activities contained within this book are designed to help you grow: it is a toolkit for piloting yourself expertly and successfully through all the experiences, opportunities, and challenges life has to offer. It's not magic, but it's like magic.

Whilst I recommend that you start with Self-Care to get a sense of where you currently are and where to focus attention, the book is designed as a pick and mix to suit you. For example, if you find that your assessment score is low for Stress Management, you may wish to begin there. If it's Mind that's flashing red, then jump into Mind first. Alternatively, you might like to go straight through, from cover to cover. The choice is yours – follow whatever path works best for you.

Make notes as you go to capture your thoughts and reflections, and do take your time. You may want to read through the book as quickly as possible, and that is OK as well. However, do remember that embedding new habits is a process over time. Therefore, take the opportunity to highlight, underline, and scribble notes wherever you need. Perhaps use the book more as an ongoing workbook to guide you through a learning journey that may take a few weeks, months, or even years.

I have found that I'm still learning, even now. Each day brings new challenges and new opportunities, different ways to test, stretch, and grow my skills. So please don't get frustrated with yourself. It takes time and patience to shift behaviour and mindset. There are false starts, U-turns, and roadblocks along the way. This is all quite normal, yet with consistency, focus, and continuous practical application over time, the results shine through. That is a promise I can make as I've seen the results in many people from different walks of life.

If you do find yourself blocked or you need an alternative view on something, please feel free to email me at deborah.hulme@minervaengagement.com and I will respond to you. It may take a week or two; however, we will connect.

Enjoy the book,
Deborah

"Self-care is giving the world the best of you instead of what's left of you."

Katie Reed

Part One

Self-Care

Introduction

We are who we are in part because of *who we are*. Our lives reflect what we do and how we behave. Whilst it can be argued that our genes have a role to play, they are only one element. In the 1990s, an international collaborative research programme was set up to map and understand all human genes. It became known as the Human Genome Project, and it led to an explosion in neuroscience research (National Human Genome Research Institute, 2022)[1].

The discoveries from the Human Genome Project inform much of our knowledge today, including an understanding that the nature/nurture domains are tightly interwoven with one another. Genes can certainly influence behaviour, physical traits, and cognitive functions. Yet at the same time, our environment, life experience, and state of wellness can directly change the level at which certain genes are expressed, which, in turn, alter both the physical structure and activity within the brain.

This is important: we may not be able to change our entire gene pool (yet), but we can alter our reality and influence our genes through how we care for ourselves, how we think, and the environment within which we stand. We can effect personal change when we understand why personal change is important as well as having access to the tools that support change.

We don't have to be a slave to our genes; we have the power within us to choose our way, how we think, and how we behave day-to-day. However, this becomes very difficult to achieve if our system is tired, stressed, and unwell. Therefore, if we want to effect successful personal change, knowing our starting point and being able to hear and understand the health updates our system sends us is hugely beneficial.

The Human Genome Project (HGP) began in 1990 and was completed in 2003. It was a groundbreaking research programme that was initiated to map all the genes in human DNA. By determining the sequence of 3 billion DNA base pairs and decoding the genetic blueprint, the programme has revolutionised biology and medicine.

With enhanced insight into different disease mechanisms, it has been possible to develop improved diagnostic tools and treatment strategies, therapies, and more personalised medicine approaches. The programme may have drawn to a close; however, its legacy continues as its findings still influence biomedical research and healthcare today.

Thrive or Survive?

To thrive rather than just survive in this modern world, looking after the self should be considered non-negotiable: a number one priority. Just as on a plane when we are instructed to put the oxygen mask on ourselves first, so we must focus on our health and wellbeing above all else – just as we need to love ourselves for others to love us; we can only be there for those around us when we are balanced and well ourselves. When operating in a state of exhaustion and high stress, we simply do not have access to the thinking or emotional resources needed to support others. Plus, our often 'hot' emotional behaviours create heightened levels of fear and uncertainty, which helps no one.

Whether we like it or not, we now live in an 'always on' culture, one that offers enormous, almost never-ending potential for opportunity, challenge, excitement, and exhaustion. So, the more we listen to what our system needs and proactively plan for rest and recovery, the more we protect our energy reserves.

Maybe when we become more robot than human, we will be able to keep going 24/7 with no negative impacts. At the time of writing though, we are still, thankfully, primarily human, albeit with some helpful mechanical interventions, such as a pacemaker or an artificial limb. Therefore, to stay well and perform well, looking after the self is not a 'nice to do', it is 100% top priority.

That's great, but where do you start? After all, there is so much information available, it's easy to feel overwhelmed and tired at even the thought of living life differently, let alone putting new ways of being into practice.

This is true, and for this reason, you will find that the Stay Well Assessment can help guide your way, along with the simplified concept of self-care unpacked into five components that you can work through in your own time.

Before we get into that though, let's just take a quick time-out for some often-neglected self-compassion.

A Moment of Self-Compassion

Many of us are quick to berate ourselves with what we should have done, or the conversation we should have had, or even the exam we should have passed. We love to 'should' all over ourselves while barely acknowledging the wonderful things we do day after day. Self-compassion is rarely practised, yet it's the foundation for self-love, and it's invaluable for an enhanced, more accurate, ongoing sense of self-worth. Therefore, before we dive into the detail of self-care, take a moment to stop and reflect on what you do well. Have a go at practising the two exercises outlined, making a habit of practising them on an ongoing basis.

Self-Reflection

During this exercise, you can either sit quietly, using the following questions as inspiration or, even better, grab a notepad and make a note of your achievements, great and small. Don't hold back; capture anything and everything that comes to mind.

- What would your friends say about you?
- What are you most proud of?
- What do you excel at?
- How do you make a difference?
- Whose life do you light up?

You might find this activity uncomfortable at first. Your brain may fight you with thoughts such as, "Why are you doing this?" or, "Stop wasting your time; this won't make any difference to you." This is perfectly normal. After years of self-flagellation, it is sometimes difficult to kickstart a new habit of self-appreciation.

Stick with it though – ignore those deceptive brain messages and continue to practise over time. I know from the many personal stories people have recounted to me that it gets easier and they become more comfortable as the new thinking pattern strengthens. It's a wonderful way to consciously recognise all the fabulous contributions you undoubtedly make every day. Plus, when you are having one of those inevitable down days, you can open your notebook or file and remind yourself of just how amazing you are.

Self-Love

Complete the mirror exercise I mentioned earlier. This one was transformational for me, and it came to me via the wonderful inspirational speaker, Lisa Nichols. Find a mirror in a quiet spot where you won't be interrupted. Look yourself in the eye in the mirror or, alternatively, use your phone (always ensure you can see your reflection). Connect with yourself as though you are your own best friend and follow the structure outlined, saying out loud:

Your Name, I am proud that you (add 3 different endings).

Your Name, I forgive you for (add 3 different endings).

Your Name, I commit to you that (add 3 different endings).

You might feel awkward; you might cry; you might want to stop – or you might smile and feel fabulous. It will be what it will be, and that is OK. You are in a room by yourself. No one else is there, so no matter the reaction, just do it.

Notice how this mirror exercise makes you feel. If you find it hard, I strongly recommend you do it for 20 or even 30 days straight (through tears if needed), and then notice how you feel at the end of the 20- or 30-day period.

Remember, deep-seated beliefs take time to shift, so remain patient with it and yourself. Keep going; create a habit of appreciating you at least once per day. Consciously notice the light that comes with loving, honouring, and caring for yourself.

The Start Point

The human system is an exquisite example of engineering, as yet unmatched by anything we as a species have developed to date. It continues to change and grow throughout its lifespan, with much of the functionality residing below the level of consciousness. Our system does not need to think how to breathe, how to repair wounds, or how to digest food; it can withstand, within reason, the heat and the cold; it can experience the quiver of excitement, and it can take itself from the joy of love to the sadness of loss in a heartbeat. Looking after that system is a top priority if we want to stay well and perform well.

No doubt there are many different elements contributing to a healthy, well self. However, from reflecting on my own experience and listening to and practising alongside others, I have found a focus on Brain, Mind, Body, Stress Management, and Social Connection delivers sustainable results over time.

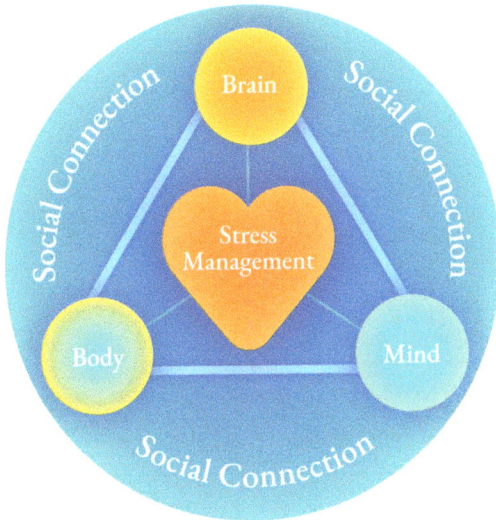

Note: *The brain and mind continuously work together. However, while some scientists and thinkers believe the brain and mind are one and cannot be separated, others disagree. For our purposes, it is helpful to think of the Brain as the physical entity composed of nerve cells and blood vessels, which can be studied, touched, and seen. Then we can think of the Mind as the mental phenomenon, with no physical structure, that enables our conscious understanding of things and forms our conscience.*

Later on, we will explore each of these components, why they are so important, and how they work together. You will also find a range of different tools and techniques that will help you develop new habits and practices for day-to-day implementation.

First though, do take a moment to complete the Stay Well Assessment. It is designed as a short exercise to help you

The Stay Well Assessment	
BRAIN	
I avoid multitasking as often as possible.	
I am comfortable resting and doing nothing.	
I take regular breaks during the day.	
I make time for play during the day.	
I am clear with others regarding my boundaries, what is ok/not ok for me.	
BRAIN: AVERAGE SCORE	
MIND	
I find it easy to avoid distractions.	
I often experience a sense of 'flow', where I lose myself in my work.	
I am conscious of my thoughts during the day.	
It is easy for me to shift from negative to positive thought patterns.	
I actively engage in positive thought habits (eg gratitude practice).	
MIND: AVERAGE SCORE	
BODY	
I regularly monitor my energy levels.	
I actively plan time for rest and recovery.	
I find it easy to sleep and I sleep well.	
I engage in regular exercise for at least 20 minutes a day.	
My daily diet is nutrient rich.	
BODY: AVERAGE SCORE	
STRESS MANAGEMENT	
I rarely experience chronic stress.	
I know how to manage my stress response.	
I understand my personal stress tolerance level.	
I recognise the triggers that activate my stress response.	
I engage in emotional regulation practices.	
STRESS MANAGEMENT: AVERAGE SCORE	
SOCIAL CONNECTION	
Quality time with friends and family is a priority for me.	
I seek out opportunities to connect with others (eg volunteering, social).	
My work/life balance is good.	
I feel well connected; loneliness is not an issue for me.	
I prioritise looking after myself to be my best self for those around me.	
SOCIAL CONNECTION: AVERAGE SCORE	

identify which of the five components may require more immediate attention from you and where to prioritise effort.

The Stay Well Assessment

Consider how balanced you are across the five components using the worksheet provided. Please answer the statements on a scale of 1 to 10 (1 meaning strongly disagree/10 meaning strongly agree with the statement). When you finish, add the totals and divide by five to find your average score for each section. Once you have worked out your average scores, add your scores to the radar chart to create your Stay Well Assessment map.

The Stay Well Radar Chart

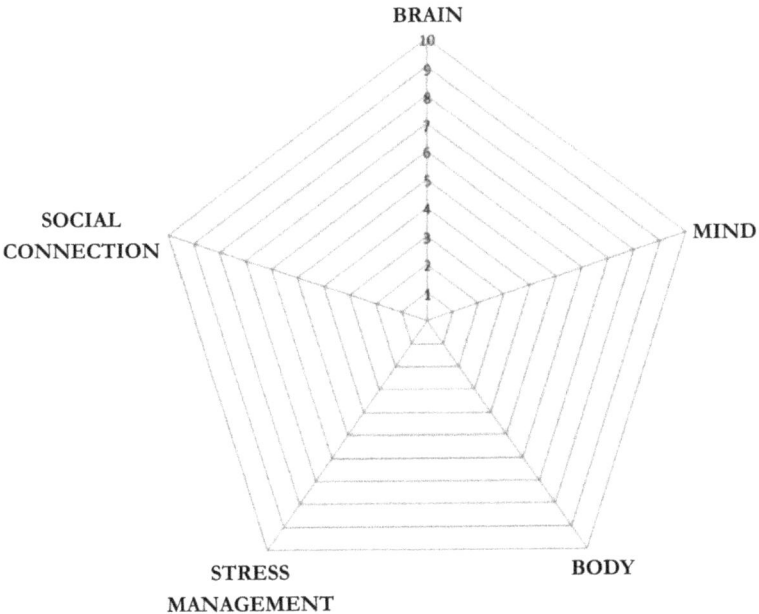

Questions for Self-Reflection

- What stands out for you when assessing your radar chart?

- Does the radar chart resonate with where you believe you need to focus attention?

- How might scores of less than 6 impact your quality of life or work activity?

Use your notebook to capture your thoughts and take a moment to reflect on your responses. Are the results surprising to you? Notice any emotion you may be feeling right now and accept that it is OK to feel that. Consider how your Self-Care state may be impacting what you do day-to-day, your relationship with friends, family, and work colleagues, and your general sense of wellbeing. Take a moment to reflect on which of the five components you might like to work on first.

Save your results somewhere safe. This is your Start Point. As you practise new habits, repeat the exercise and notice how and where your radar chart shifts. It's a good way of monitoring progress over time and keeping track of what you may need to upweight, change, or adapt to remain in balance and stay well.

Manage the Energy

With a deeper understanding of where to focus attention, can we get started?

Not quite!

Move forward if you would like to; however, it is always wise to understand how much energy we have available for a habit or behaviour change before we start to work on ourselves. Change requires effort over time, and if we're already exhausted, we simply don't have the internal resources available to sustain the effort for long enough.

Before we start, it may be necessary to make some adjustments to our daily routines, creating space for rest and recovery. Otherwise, we're in danger of putting additional strain on our system, generating increased anxiety, while reducing energy levels even further. This will not deliver a good outcome, and may even make things worse.

I use the energy bucket to help me understand where my energy reserves might be at any given time. It's a useful analogy: the bucket represents the human system and the water level equals available energy. The tap found at the bottom of the bucket can never be turned off; it's always leaking, and the same applies in life. The human system is always leaking energy, when we sleep, when we breathe, and for everything we do, 24/7. For us to stay well, the ratio between energy in and energy out must remain in balance.

When we look after ourselves, allowing time for rest and recovery, and things run smoothly day-to-day, this is relatively easy to do. However, when we don't stop, when we face change, challenges, or unexpected events, it becomes more difficult. Therefore, to remain in balance, we must develop a heightened awareness of our energy level, becoming more proactive around energy-in activities, thereby compensating for the speed of energy draining out. If energy levels settle below the tap, it becomes much more of an effort to rebalance.

Allow yourself some time to work around the bucket, and capture on the page or in your notebook, what might be impacting your energy levels, positively and/or negatively. Consider whether you are in-balance or running on empty. You might want to reference the following questions to stimulate your reflections.

The Energy Bucket

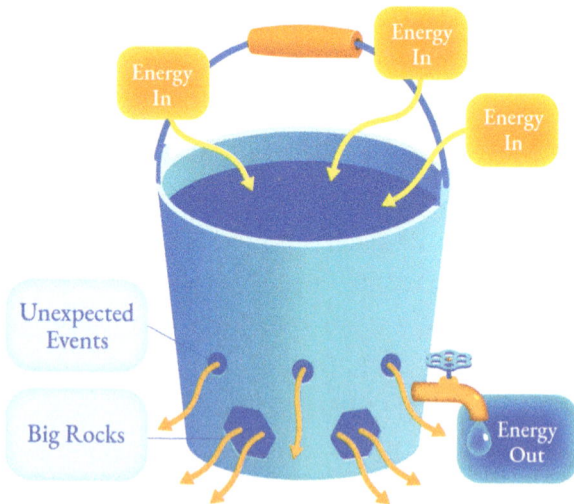

Adapted from Brabban and Turkington, 2002

- **Energy In** – energy enhancers, eg socialising, sleep, exercise, work, rest.

- **Energy Out** – energy drainers, eg work, family, exercise, conflict.

- **Big Rocks** – big events which dramatically drain energy levels, eg a promotion, moving house, divorce, ill-health. Big Rocks can have a timespan of just one day to several years. For example, Covid-19 bashed a huge hole in many of our buckets. We lived with this Big Rock for over two years, and for some of us, it's still ongoing.

- **Unexpected Events** – small, annoying things that drain energy, eg a flat tyre, lost keys, a water leak, a stolen phone, or cancelled meetings. They punch smaller holes which, while not on the scale of Big Rocks, still drain energy, albeit at a slower rate.

Note: Activities that contribute to energy-in or energy-out are not mutually exclusive. For example, we may receive a huge energy boost socialising with friends; however, talking and connecting will also use energy. We may feel energised after exercise, yet to exercise, we will use energy.

Once you've completed the energy bucket activity, listing Energy-In, Energy-Out, any Big Rocks, and Unexpected Events impacting your energy level, consider the following questions. They may prompt further reflection and awareness.

- What are the biggest drains on my energy?
- What impact does this have on me?
- What are the signs that I need to refill my bucket?
- Who helps me to refill my bucket?
- What helps me refill my bucket?
- What benefits do I experience when I am fully energised?

- What do people around me notice when I am fully energised?

- What do I do each day or week to restore and renew myself?

I've used this exercise across many in-person and online workshops, and it invariably produces a plethora of lightbulb moments. Take your time with it and remain present to the fact that many of us are running on empty, while, at the same time, beating ourselves up for not doing enough. Worse than this, we beat ourselves up even more for becoming emotional, experiencing foggy thinking, or just generally finding it hard to cope.

Considering how the world is spinning right now, it's not even surprising. If you find that your energy is depleted, it is understandable, acceptable, and not that unusual. Take a breath, remember the importance of self-compassion, and think through the small steps you can take to create more rest and recovery time to refill your energy reserves.

In Summary

Now you understand where you may need to focus your attention and have assessed your current energy levels, you have the insight you need to prioritise where you want to start. If you are low on energy, consider how best to enable rest and recovery for your system. It will be difficult to work on the activities and practices if you are exhausted to begin with.

With energy levels at least partially restored, work through the book in a way that suits you. It does not need to be a linear read. You can start exactly where you are. Whatever works for you is the right way to go, and remember:

- We may not be able to change our entire gene pool, but we can influence gene expression via a balance of thought, behaviour, and environment.

- Caring for the self is a combination of Brain, Mind, Body, and Stress Management, situated within the context of Social Connection.

- To thrive in a modern fast-moving world, looking after the self is not a 'nice to have' – it's the number one top priority.

- Don't underestimate the importance of self-compassion and recognising the wonderful things we do every day. Develop a helpful habit of taking a moment every day to practise self-compassion.

- Use your Stay-Well Radar Chart to check progress over time and prioritise where to focus attention.

- Check out those energy levels, and if you're exhausted, build in some much-needed rest and recovery time. An exhausted system does not have the resources to adopt new habits, change, or adapt.

"The brain was constructed to change."

Dr Michael Merzenich

Part Two

Brain

Introduction

*I*t sounds crazy to me now, but I honestly never used to think much about my brain. I had this belief that the brain I was born with was fixed and pretty much looked after itself. My intelligence, ability to change, learn, and grow had been determined at birth, and I had to live as best I could with what I had been given. This thought extended out to my personality and behaviours, which were, to me, permanent and unchanging. The old saying, "A leopard can't change its spots," made perfect sense to me, and I remember using that quote in my earlier years, both for myself and when describing others. As it turns out, I am not the only one to think this way.

For centuries, the brain has been unappreciated for the complex organ it is. If we go back in time, the ancient Egyptians used to throw the brain away, whilst preserving the more important heart and other selected organs during the mummification process. The Greek philosopher Aristotle believed the heart to be the location of intelligence, while the brain worked as a type of radiator, keeping the all-important heart from overheating.

Indeed, it was only in the late 20th century with developing technology and advances in science – plus the explosion of research that came with the Human Genome Project – that we really began to understand more about the brain and, in particular, the intimate relationship that exists between brain, mind, and body.

For me, this knowledge was joyous. It opened all sorts of possibilities and opportunities for alternative ways of being, thinking, and doing: change that I'd always believed to be outside my grasp was now suddenly a reality. I was not destined to be the same person, with the same intelligence, the same emotional responses, and the same mindset throughout my entire life. I could direct who I wanted to be, grow my intelligence, and learn how to regulate and develop my personality over time. This wonderful brain of mine could structure and restructure itself repeatedly in response to my learning, my thinking, and the environment within which I put myself.

The brain is a soft and buttery mass of tissue made up of about 78% water. It accounts for 2% of our body weight, uses 20% of our internal resources (glucose and oxygen), and burns roughly 20% to 30% of all the calories we consume. It is intimately connected to the body and significantly influences our overall sense of health and wellbeing. Everything we do, from heart rate and emotion, to learning and memory, starts with a chemical reaction in the brain (Ampel, Muraven and McNay 2018)[1].

Continual Learning

In fact, the more we continue to learn, stretch, and grow throughout life, the healthier the brain becomes because it continues to generate more and more connections between neurons. If we were to open the brain of an 80-year-old person who had continued to learn new hobbies, develop new skills, and explore new experiences, we would see a mass of neural connections, with a density similar to that of the Amazon Forest. Conversely, if that same 80-year-old had instead passed the years sitting on the sofa watching television, with little or no stimulating interaction, then the connections within that same brain would be sparse in nature, more akin to a lone tree standing in the middle of a desert. Basically, if we don't use it, we lose it.

A neural connection is like a bridge between brain cells known as neurons. It's where the neurons use electricity and chemicals to pass messages and talk to one another. These connections enable the brain to do a variety of things including thinking, moving, and feeling (Anon, n.d.)[2].

'If we don't use it, we lose it.'

That is not to say it's easy. When we learn something new, change a behaviour, or even alter the way we think about something, we must first create a new pathway or mental map in the brain. This is an effortful process which demands a combination of focused attention and deliberate practice. As the new pathways take shape in the brain, the learning or change process can feel hard, slow, and challenging. It is often exhausting. Yet, if we preserve and keep going when it gets tough, then the new pathways do form, and change happens. The struggle is necessary as it is precisely from the struggle that learning and change emerges.

The Magic of Change

The brain changes itself by a process known as neuroplasticity. That sounds complicated, but neuroplasticity simply refers to the brain's ability to form new connections and pathways: *neuro* refers to the neurons that form the building blocks of the brain and nervous system; *plasticity* to the brain's ability to restructure itself. Indeed, the brain can restructure or change itself in three different ways.

- **Chemical:** the brain increases or decreases chemical interaction between neurons, dependent on what we are doing or focusing our attention on.

- **Structural:** the physical structure of the brain changes because of the environment we are in, the learning we undertake, or our repetitive thought patterns.

- **Functional:** the brain moves some of its functionality from a damaged area of the brain to an undamaged area for relearning opportunities – for example, regaining the use of a limb or reallocating aspects of the visual cortex to sharpen auditory functionality.

From a personal development perspective, it is chemical and structural neuroplasticity that offers the greatest opportunity

The Moken are a seafaring people who inhabit areas along the coasts of Myanmar and Thailand, and they live as hunter-gatherers. They spend a great deal of time in boats because they harvest tiny shellfish and other food off the seabed, sometimes at depths as low as 23 metres (75ft). They do this without scuba equipment or masks. A study by Dr Anna Gislén (Gislén et al., 2003)[3] from Lund University in Sweden has shown that Moken children have underwater vision twice as good as European children of the same age.

In her study, Dr Gislén found no differences in the children's respective eye structures or in their vision on land, only when underwater. The secret to the Moken children's abilities lies in the way their eyes have adapted to the underwater environment. When they are in the ocean, their pupils constrict by 22%, overruling the automatic reflex we all normally have to open the pupil when underwater. This allows the Moken children to see twice as well underwater, and it is a wonderful example of how the brain adapts the body to suit its needs.

Neuroscientists believe that anyone can learn how to see better underwater, it just takes practice and time. If you would like to see how the pupil constricts in reality, open the link https://www.youtube.com/watch?v=YIKm3Pq9U8M when next on your browser.

for growth and change. Every time we focus on learning or changing something, we activate an alternative firing pattern between certain neurons which creates the beginnings of a new pathway in the brain. As we focus attention on what we want to achieve, the newly formed firing pattern increases in strength and speed with each repetition, further embedding the learning or change we want to make. It's a process commonly known as Hebb's law.

Hebb's Law

Hebb's law or Hebbian theory emerged from the work of Donald Hebb, a Canadian neuropsychologist, in 1949 (Hebb, 1949)[4]. It describes how changes occur in the brain in response to the repeated and continuous firing of certain neurons. It's often summarised as "cells that fire together, wire together."

Essentially, as neurons are repeatedly activated in the same pattern, they eventually form an ingrained brain circuit. Once the circuit has become ingrained through repetition and practice, the brain areas involved in that circuit then respond effortlessly in the same way every time a similar situation arises.

"Cells that fire together, wire together"

As an example, this is when we move from clunky, hard-on-the-ears piano lessons to fluid piano playing in a performance.

The critical ingredient or glue necessary to activate neurons is focused attention. Quite simply, without focused attention, no change takes place. When we focus attention on whatever it is we are trying to do, neurons activate and connect into a pattern, which is the first step towards the creation of an ingrained circuit. What's even more amazing is how signal speed within the brain increases and stabilises around the forming circuit. This is because the more we practise and repeat, the more the brain wraps a protective coating around the circuit.

The Myelin Sheath

The formal name for this protective coating is myelin sheath (Morell and Quarles, 2017)[5], and it can be likened to the white plastic coating we see wrapped around copper wires. But within our brain, it acts as a speed booster for our brain signals. The more myelin coating there is, the faster the brain signal travels. In terms of processing speed, the myelin sheath can help you progress from an old-fashioned finger dial phone right up to the power of 5G.

Myelin is crucial for learning and improving skills because it strengthens and speeds up brain connection and communication. Focused attention activates neurons in the brain to form a pattern of firing, then, the more we continue to practise and repeat, the more myelin the brain builds, stabilising the pathway until it becomes a fully ingrained circuit.

The Myelin Sheath

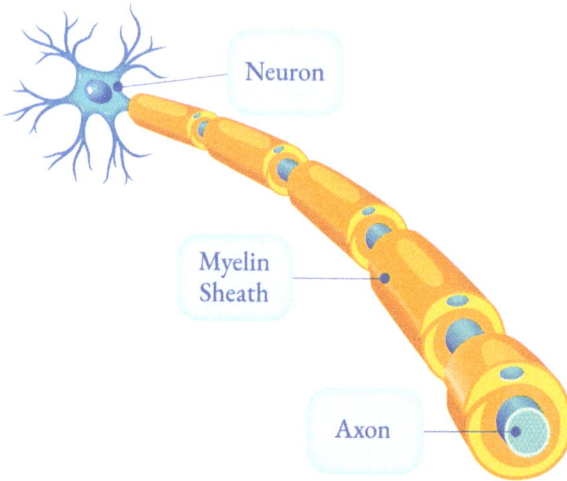

Neuron

Myelin
Sheath

Axon

Attentional Focus

What we pay attention to matters, and understanding how the brain change process works is powerful. With the right knowledge, we can intentionally direct how our brain reshapes itself, creating alternative, more constructive thinking and behaviour patterns. The more we focus and apply consistent deliberate practice, the more these newly formed pathways are strengthened, until they become firmly embedded as a new learning, a permanent habit, or a changed way of being.

What is extremely important to note is that the brain makes no judgment on how it changes. It has no moral code; it simply restructures itself according to what we are focusing our attention on. That is to say if we engage in repeated patterns of complaining, the brain will create a new pathway to facilitate increased complaining. As we repeat this behaviour and focus on complaining, the brain strengthens that pathway until a deeply embedded complaining habit has become the default behaviour. Alternatively, if we focus attention on what we enjoy and what we are grateful for, the brain will strengthen that pathway instead. The brain can restructure itself towards either the positive or negative – how it shapes itself is within our gift to direct.

'The brain has no moral code.'

It is true that the brain can change itself quicker and faster during childhood than in adulthood, which is why it is so much easier to learn a new language as a child. However, while the process may slow as we age, the fundamentals of focused attention and deliberate ongoing practice remain the same. For this reason, as we age, the need to continue learning new things becomes more important rather than less important if we want to remain active and vibrant.

Thanks to the way the brain changes, the more we sit on a chair and strengthen the connection for sitting, the harder, over time, we will find it to get off the chair and walk. The more we stop thinking through complex challenges, weakening those connections, the less we will be able to think through complex challenges. Simply put, the more we engage in new learning opportunities, the more connections the brain makes and the denser and healthier it becomes.

Therefore, regardless of age, never shy away from new challenges or learning opportunities – whether they be a new crossword, learning a new language, exploring new places, or getting lost in a fabulous new hobby. The more we learn and understand about the brain, including the magic of change, the more we can manage ourselves better to stay well and perform well.

"Because of the power of neuroplasticity, you can, in fact, reframe your world and rewire your brain so that you are more objective. You have the power to see things as they are so that you can respond thoughtfully, deliberately, and effectively to everything you experience."

Elizabeth Thornton

An Effortful Process

Whatever we do today structures the brain of tomorrow. There are different ways we can enhance and direct change in the brain; this could be through learning, repetition, meditation, visualisation and/or exercise. However, it's important to recognise that change does not happen overnight; it takes time and ongoing practice.

The brain area necessary to focus attention sits just behind the forehead. It's known as the prefrontal cortex, and it is often referred to as the executive centre. This area of the brain is responsible for conscious thinking and decision-making, and it differentiates us from the rest of the animal kingdom. The executive centre is an amazing piece of kit which is involved in complex tasks such as problem-solving and controlling impulses. Because of this, the executive centre demands a lot of fuel to function, more than other regions of the brain. When it functions, it gets hungry, gobbling up available glucose (sugar) and oxygen to keep going. For this reason, the brain will only engage the executive centre when absolutely necessary.

This is important, because from a brain changeability perspective, we need to engage the executive centre to focus the attention necessary to create new brain pathways for change. If we are in balance, rested, and not overly stressed, the brain has the internal resources (glucose and oxygen) available to facilitate this. However, if we are tired, overwhelmed, anxious, or worse, chronically stressed, we just do not have the resources needed to focus attention, meaning that we are then unable to establish the brain pathways necessary for change.

It is also important to note that because the executive centre requires high levels of internal energy to function, even when the internal resources are available to focus attention, we tire easily. Hence the importance of regular breaks to get the blood and oxygen flowing, along with good nutrition to refill the used glucose stores. In other words, when we are learning something new or experiencing change, there is a heightened requirement to be kind to ourselves and to look after ourselves, which is something many of us overlook.

Take a moment to reflect on the last time you learned something new or wanted to change the way you did something.

- Was it right first time or slow and clunky to start?
- How tired were you after each learning session?
- With practice, did the learning process gather speed as the brain circuits developed?
- Was it easier on certain days or times and, if so, can you recognise why?

- Knowing what you know now, what might you do differently to better support your brain to learn, change, and adapt in the future?

Note: Don't underestimate the importance of using visualisation during the learning/change process. Visualisation and real-world learning trigger the same brain regions with both options resulting in the creation and strengthening of neural connections (Lacourse, Orr and Turner, 2003)[6]. When we visualise, it's as though we are practising live and it's just as effective. The only difference being we can visualise anywhere, anytime – we don't need to have the instrument, ball, racket, book, PC, or anything else to hand. Visualisation is a great way to speed up the learning process.

Before we move on, I want to talk about multitasking, which is something many of us do. We are often even proud and eager to demonstrate how well we do it. Unfortunately, that also means many of us are party to a collective form of delusion. In reality, we don't multitask, and when we attempt it, we suffer from making an increased number of mistakes, while at the same time, rapidly depleting the very resources needed to create new pathways for change.

The Myth of Multitasking

The view that we can effectively multitask is largely a myth (Cleveland Clinic, 2021)[7]. We do not have the mental capacity to consciously focus on two things at once. Contrary to popular belief, very few of us can successfully multitask. Most of us multi-switch: we switch between different tasks so quickly that we perceive the action as being simultaneous when it is not. This multi-switching is effortful and quickly drains the energy-hungry executive centre of the brain. It can work well, but for most of us it is only effective when one of the actions we are undertaking is so automatic we don't have to consciously think about it.

Consider a time when you drove home thinking about a work challenge or personal conundrum. On your arrival at home, you suddenly notice that you can't remember anything about the drive – not the lights; not the roundabouts; overtaking – nothing. In this situation your conscious thought was fully occupied with the challenge or conundrum you were considering. While your prefrontal cortex was occupied by your conscious thought, the car was actually being driven by your habitual brain, following the deeply embedded and fully automatic driving circuit already firmly in place.

Another example might be the ability to touch-type and read text at the same time. We can only do this, though, when touch-typing is already an embedded circuit, freeing up the brain's resources to concentrate on reading text. When the touch-typing is not automatic, the typing speed is slower and the error rate is higher because now we must multi-switch between reading, typing, reading, typing, reading, typing.

There's also clear evidence that multi-switching increases the production of cortisol as well as adrenaline. Too much of these hormones can overstimulate the brain and cause mental fog, stress, and scrambled thinking. Some research (American Psychological Association, 2006)[8] indicates that this form of multi-switching can reduce productivity by approximately 40%. Now, that is a big drop.

You might be wondering if anyone can multitask? Well, according to Professor David Strayer, Director of the Applied Cognition Lab at the University of Utah (Watson and Strayer, 2010)[9], the answer is yes – although multitaskers account for less than an estimated 3% of the global population. For this small proportion of the world, their ability to multitask is due to their brain being structured differently from birth. They were born that way.

For the rest of us, multitasking is just a drain on the brain. It is far better to focus on one thing at a time. This is particularly so because, once interrupted, it is said to take between 8 and 25 minutes to return fully to where we were before the interruption (The Impact of Interruptions | People & Culture)[10]. If that were not enough, if we engage in regular multitasking, which is in fact multi-switching for most of us, we find it harder and harder to focus the crucial attention needed for change. The ability to focus and think deeply is critical to high performance and yet often unknowingly, we train ourselves to do the exact opposite, multi-switching our way through the day.

Brain Health

Housed within a hard shell that has many sharp, bony ridges on the inside, the brain, with its buttery texture, is relatively easy to damage, hence the ongoing and increasingly vocal discussion that's now taking place about the safety of contact sports where play can impact the head and skull. During 2019, the Scottish Youth Football Association stopped children under the age of 11 from heading the ball. This was in response to research findings from the University of Glasgow (Russell et al, 2019)[11] which suggested that former professional football players were three and a half times more likely to die of degenerative brain disorders than people of the same age range in the general population.

Jump forward to 2023, and nearly 300 rugby players, including World Cup winners, are currently in the process of taking the governing bodies of World Rugby, England Rugby Football Union, and Welsh Rugby Union to court for brain damage sustained while playing rugby. The results of the case are not known at the time of writing; however, we do know that the players are suffering from a mix of neurological complications associated with the contact nature of rugby.

The key takeaway from these examples is the need to protect the head as much as possible with appropriate helmets and specialised headgear when engaging in certain activities, sports, or work situations. Bumps and bangs to the head can result in physical damage; however, they can also cause unexpected behavioural or emotional shifts. Protection in certain situations should always be non-negotiable.

The impact of physical knocks and shocks to the head are becoming more understood and mainstream, but we should not underestimate the less obvious signs of poor brain health. It may be locked inside the skull, but the brain has different ways and means to let us know when it needs attention. Our challenge is to listen to what it is trying to tell us, taking the necessary steps to protect brain health if we want to stay well and perform well.

Foggy Brain

When we are unable to think clearly, when thoughts are muddled, slow, or it's difficult to recall details and process information, we are likely in the grip of what is often referred to as foggy brain – a descriptive catch-all name for when the brain is not functioning as well as it should. I know many people, particularly within the corporate world, who report experiencing foggy brain, yet just keep on pushing through, hoping it will get better. Well, it can get better, but not without change. Doing nothing is not the answer.

Foggy brain manifests in different ways. It can result from a plethora of underlying causes such as lack of exercise, poor sleep habits, chronic stress, hormonal changes, a poor diet, or even exposure to toxins and pollutants. Any and all of these negatively impact brain health, contributing to foggy brain.

Remember, the brain uses an estimated 20% of our available internal energy resources. If those resources are not being replenished through good sleep, or are often rapidly depleted due to chronic stress, then we simply do not have the brain capacity available to think clearly. This makes complex processing such as planning and decision-making incredibly difficult to do. Finding the actual cause of foggy brain is a process of self-awareness and reflection. You might want to begin by reflecting on the following questions:

- Am I getting enough quality sleep – waking up and going to bed at consistent times?

- Am I eating a healthy, nutritionally balanced diet?

- Am I staying hydrated throughout the day?

- Am I getting enough exercise?

- Am I managing my stress levels effectively?

- Am I spending too much time in front of a screen?

- Do I need to reassess my alcohol, caffeine, or tobacco intake?

If you answered yes to any of the above questions, or any other contributory factors sprang to mind, consider what you can do or the actions you can take to readdress the balance. Don't forget to make a note of what works and what does not work in your notebook. This is a helpful habit to cultivate, making it easier over time to identify the main factors contributing to foggy brain.

Poor Memory Function

Memory function varies from person to person, and processing speed and information recall can also decline with age. Certainly, when memory starts to falter, our first thoughts tend to gravitate towards dementia and Alzheimer's. While this should always be checked by a doctor, it is worth noting that chronic long-term stress also has a significant impact on memory function.

There is a structure in the brain known as the hippocampus, which among other things is fundamental for transferring short-term memory to long-term memory. When in a chronic long-term stress state, we produce exceptionally high levels of the stress hormone, cortisol. In this situation, the increased cortisol levels act like poison on the hippocampus, destroying neurons and negatively impacting its ability to transfer memory.

The good news is that the hippocampus is an area of the brain where neurons have the potential to regenerate. When we address the cause of the chronic stress, the hippocampus may produce new neurons through a process called neurogenesis, supporting the repairing and restoring of memory functionality. While unexpected memory changes should never be ignored, they can signal an overstressed brain, prompting the need to consider existing stress levels. You will find more information on how to better manage your stress response, using different tools and techniques, in Part 5, Stress Management.

Overwhelm

Feeling overwhelmed and out of control is not comfortable, and it is hardly surprising that we find ourselves in this state when we consider the numerous distractions, interactions, 24/7 news bulletins, and social media feeds we deal with every day. That's not forgetting looking after family members, caring for the sick, or holding down a job. It never stops! Yet like it or not, to stay well, the brain must rest.

If you force it to keep going, it starts to malfunction. This shows itself in many ways. We may become emotional over the smallest of things with outbursts of inappropriate anger, upset, or even jollity. Often, there is so much swimming through our mind, but we just can't get started on what really matters. We end up procrastinating, focused on all the wrong things. It becomes a vicious circle. When we feel overwhelmed, the inclination is to run faster in order to cope, but this then results in more overwhelm, and the need to run even faster.

As counterintuitive as it may seem, the answer is to stop: to build in time for rest and recovery, thus allowing the brain to unscramble itself, work through what needs to be done, by when, and then move forward one step at a time.

An easy win is to get all that noise out of your head and onto paper or the laptop/tablet/phone – whichever takes your fancy. Make a list of everything you need to do, chunk it up, and prioritise the list. It is much easier to work with information when it's out of your head. The brain only has a small stage with which to work through conscious thought, and consequently, it's easily overwhelmed if left to its own devices.

Plus, when it's out of your head, it's much easier to see what needs doing, what activity we can trim, trash, or transfer to someone else so we can free up some precious space. Get into radical prioritisation mode and cut out everything that is not urgent or does not need to be done now or ever. Again, don't forget to check in with yourself. When we are tired, hungry, or overstressed, even the smallest of things that we can normally easily cope with become difficult and overwhelming.

A harder habit to cultivate is saying No. The thought of saying No is often so fear inducing that we say Yes to please others, even if it means we are exhausting and overloading ourselves.

And we do end up overloading ourselves, to the point that we often become resentful, argumentative, or depressed, eventually collapsing under the strain of it, which is not good for ourselves or those around us. Learning to say No, is an art, and yes, it's uncomfortable to begin with, but it does get easier with practice. Try putting the decision back onto the other person with some robust consequence management, for example:

- Yes, of course I can do that for you; however, it means that I won't be able to take you to the football match you wanted to go to. What would you prefer to do?

- I've already committed to delivering X by Y, which means if I do take on your request, I won't get it back to you until Z. Does that work for you? If not, you may prefer to ask someone else.

One of the essential components of saying No is being clear about your own boundaries, the dividing lines that separate your thoughts, feelings, needs, and personal space from others. Boundaries play an important role in managing overwhelm, but of course, it is not easy. It took me almost half a lifetime to understand the importance of boundaries, so I can understand why so many people have neither identified nor communicated their personal boundaries to others.

Clarify the Boundaries

Setting boundaries, understanding what is OK and not OK for us, is not a selfish act. I would actually argue quite the opposite because the more we set boundaries, the more we protect our own energy and vitality, therefore the more we can be there for those around us. In fact, this is supported by research undertaken by American professor and writer, Brené Brown, who found that leaders with the healthiest boundaries were able to display heightened levels of empathy for those around them, as well as being more respectful of the boundaries set by other people (Brené Brown, n.d)[12].

The setting and maintaining of healthy boundaries establishes clear limits regarding what we are willing to accept in terms of demands, expectations, and requests from others. We can disagree with someone while being clear that screaming and shouting is unacceptable; we can clarify that we can work overtime while stating that this must not become the norm; we can empathise with a friend's trauma while making sure we do not take on the drama ourselves.

Being clear on our boundaries gives us permission to say No when needed, lowering the risk of overwhelm and cognitive overload, while at the same time improving relationships and supporting wellbeing in general.

Boundaries themselves can take different forms:

- **physical** – defining our level of comfort with physical contact
- **time related** – clarifying the hours we are prepared to dedicate to a task or activity
- **material** – setting limits on what we are prepared to share or lend

- **emotional** – being clear about how much emotional burden we can carry on behalf of others

Boundaries can also vary from person to person, dependent on cultural, social, and individual factors. When they are well considered, structured, and communicated, boundaries act like an internal compass, ensuring we don't lose ourselves as we struggle to meet the demands of everyone else. As we learn to identify and respect personal needs and limits, our self-esteem and confidence grow, and we find we are more available and present for those around us.

Boundary Considerations

If you have never thought about boundaries before, you might like to consider the following questions to prompt your thoughts and reflect on whether establishing or strengthening boundaries would be helpful for you.

1. Defining and preparing for setting clear boundaries

Take a moment to clarify your understanding of a boundary and what it means to you.

- What is your understanding and definition of a boundary?
- What do you expect to happen when you identify your boundaries?
- What has stopped you putting boundaries in place to date?
- What obstacles do you anticipate when clarifying and communicating your boundaries?
- What can you put in place to reduce those obstacles?

2. Visualise and name your limits.

When thinking about your boundaries, you might want to consider:

- What is causing unnecessary stress and discomfort?
- What do you look forward to each day versus what you dread?
- Who or what gives you energy?
- What areas of your work completely exhaust you?
- What makes you feel safe, supported, and valued?
- To live according to your values, what boundaries do you need to establish?
- Why is this important to you?

3. If you are consistently doing too much...

Reflect on how you can change or create new boundaries for the week and months ahead. As a prompt consider:

- Are you spending too little or too much time at home?
- Have you said Yes to too many things?
- Is your day structured and organised to work for you? If not, what needs to change?
- Have you communicated your current workload clearly to those around you?
- Do you need a check-in with your family/team/colleagues to establish the priorities?
- Do your family/team/colleagues know and appreciate everything else you are doing?

Setting Boundaries

Once you have established for yourself that boundaries may be helpful, use the worksheet provided to:

- identify the boundaries that work for you.

- plan out how best to communicate your boundaries to others.

- consider how to handle any objections arising.

Boundary Worksheet

When working on your boundaries, be specific. Imagine scenarios, people involved, potential reactions, etc.

Break this down into segments and map out a plan of action, identifying what to do when faced with challenges.

My Boundary	Why is it important? What are the benefits?	Who do I need to communicate my boundary to?	What hurdles or objections might I encounter?	How will I handle any objections?	What resources or support can I rely on to set and protect the boundary?
Example: I don't respond to emails after 7pm.	Example: I want to spend quality time with my family before bedtime.	Example: My manager and my team.	Example: My team has a habit of sending evening emails. They may not respond well to my request.	Example: Explain the importance of family to my productivity and wellbeing. Provide a number for emergency use after 6.30pm.	Example: Speak to my manager regarding the importance of this for me. Keep checking in with my team to ensure we iron out any early wrinkles.

Brain Basics

Many of us live almost non-stop lives, bouncing between work, social, and family commitments. A well-balanced, rested, and cared for brain gives us a much better chance to thrive rather than just survive our way through life's eclectic mix of challenges and opportunities. With a basic understanding of the brain's needs, which are surprisingly straightforward, we can really move the dial on brain health, reaping the benefit as we invest in supporting, protecting, and enhancing brain functionality.

Sleep

Sleep is how the brain restores itself and is crucial for brain health (Worley, 2018)[13]. During sleep, certain areas of the brain are more active than when we are awake because it works to make sense of the waking hours. Overnight, the brain works to enhance the process of neuroplasticity while consolidating learning and memories, often popping insights and answers we did not previously have access to into our conscious mind, ready for us to take action on waking.

When we are asleep, our brain also completes several toxin wash cycles, flushing out natural toxins to bring brain toxicity back to healthy levels. Indeed, there is a lot written these days about poor sleep habits and the impact this has on memory, creativity, and the ability to think logically. Now, there is research highlighting the link between lack of sleep and neurodegenerative conditions such as Alzheimer's and even obesity (Bryant, 2021)[14].

While ongoing research is clearly necessary – and, yes, we do need to continue expanding our knowledge – I sometimes think we frighten ourselves so much that the stress makes it even harder to sleep. I know when I was suffering from a bad dose of insomnia, it was an awful experience. There were three things that saved me:

1. I stopped telling myself I could not sleep. I remembered that the mind is powerful. If I keep telling myself I can't sleep, then I won't sleep, so I stopped sending those signals: I changed the narrative.

2. I became rigid with my sleep-wake cycle. I went to bed at the same time every night and got up at the same time every morning, regardless of whether I slept or not, and I had no naps during the day. The first 10 days were horrible, but then I started to sleep when I went to bed, sleeping longer without interruption before I woke up.

3. I found my optimum sleep time. I need 8 hours – no more. If I go to bed at 10pm, then I wake at 6.30am, so there is no point beating myself up if I don't sleep until 7am. Some of us need 9 hours, some of us only 7 hours. A tiny minority are said to function well on less than 7 hours, but that is because they are wired differently, not because they trained themselves to do it (Tossell et al., 2023)[15].

Of course, I did other things like keeping the room cool and dark. I made sure I got out into the daylight before 10am, setting my circadian rhythm to release melatonin 12 to 14 hours later (Mead, 2008)[16]. However, the three things listed previously helped me the most.

Sleeping well is not a given. Some of us must work at it harder than others, particularly as we get older. So, if you do find sleep difficult, stop telling yourself you can't sleep; be kind to yourself; take it one step at a time. If all else fails, book to see a CBTi specialist: a cognitive behavioural therapy expert who specialises in sleep.

Eat

The brain is extremely active, demanding a high percentage of the overall daily energy requirement supplied by food. For infants, 87% of the daily energy intake supplies the brain. In children between the ages of 6 and 12, 30% to 45% of their energy is utilised in the brain, and by adulthood, the energy demands of the brain settles to around 20% to 25% (Kuzawa, C., & Blair, C. 2019)[17].

Poor nutrition can indirectly lead to reduced performance by exacerbating stress, sleep disturbances, and general fatigue, all of which impact our sense of wellbeing. Sustained brain power relies on a varied diet of nutrient rich foods. As such, the brain requires a steady supply of essential nutrients, such as omega-3 fatty acids, antioxidants, vitamins, and minerals, to function well. Foods rich in these nutrients include fatty fish, like salmon and trout; leafy greens; berries; nuts; and whole grains, whereas high-sugar, high-fat processed foods have a negative impact on brain function. An adverse change in mental function is one of the primary signals of nutrient deficiency (Muscaritoli, 2021)[18].

Exercise

Exercise doesn't recharge the brain in the same way as sleep and food, but it hugely contributes to overall brain health. Physical exercise is great for the body and the brain. A single workout will improve our mood: research into the effects of physical exercise for individuals diagnosed with attention deficit hyperactivity disorder (ADHD) indicates that we have the ability to sustain attention for at least two hours after 30 minutes of exercise (Rassovsky and Alfassi, 2019)[19]. In addition, sustained exercise over the long-term changes the brain's anatomy, physiology, and function. Long-term exercise strengthens the ability to focus and pay attention, while also improving memory function (Roig et al., 2013)[20].

The more we exercise, the stronger our brain becomes, which reduces our susceptibility to neurodegenerative diseases and diminishes the effect of cognitive decline from aging. Thirty minutes of exercise three or four times a week is enough, and we don't have to make special trips to the gym or the pool. Exercise is more sustainable when worked into daily life. For example, we can walk up the stairs rather than standing on the escalator or taking the lift; we can walk to the local shop and leave the car in the garage; or we can just ramp up the music and jump about in the kitchen for 10 minutes.

Stimulation and Challenge

Challenging activities such as puzzles, crosswords, reading, learning a new language, or playing musical instruments all help create new neural connections and strengthen existing ones, which enhances your memory, problem-solving skills, and creativity (Aliyari et al., 2022)[21].

Notice that we say challenging activities: the brain loves challenge. We need to stretch to grow, which can be uncomfortable at times; however, stretching to the point of overwhelm should be avoided. Overwhelm activates the stress response, increases anxiety, and effectively cancels out all the benefits that you're working hard to gain. If whatever you are doing starts to feel overwhelming, the best way forward is to map out the task on paper or your laptop, chunk it up into smaller more manageable steps, and then move forward one action at a time.

Energy

For the brain to work well, it needs a balanced combination of daily activity: focused work, play, rest, exercise, connection, and sleep. Internal energy oscillates in 90-minute cycles, and the brain benefits from a break period on cycle completion. Understanding the internal energy flow helps us use the energy available to us more intelligently (Gorvett, 2019)[22].

For example, we can apply the 80/20 rule to our internal energy consumption. That means moving low value tasks to align with low energy periods. We can also take more regular breaks, even if it's for a quick stretch, at least every 90 minutes or so. The important point is that we can't just keep going. Managing our internal energy, rest, and having short breaks are as important to high performance as continual learning and skills development.

The Brain: Fun Facts

Highly connected with huge storage capacity

The brain has around 86 billion neurons. There are more potential connections between the neurons than there are stars in the universe. It has a storage capacity for 300 years' worth of TV shows (Synap.ac, n.d.)[23].

Compact structure

The wrinkled appearance of the brain is made up of ridges and canals called gyri and sulci. If laid flat with the wrinkles smoothed out, the cerebral cortex would cover an area of about 2,300 sq cm (Guan et al., 2022)[24]. This large surface area enables the more complex tasks.

Takes 25 years to build

The process of building a brain takes about 25 years, and the prefrontal cortex – the area that sits just behind the forehead – is the last part to fully develop (Wnuk, 2018)[25].

Environment has a significant impact on brain development

Without an environment of emotional care and cognitive stimulation, the human brain cannot develop normally. A caring environment is particularly important during infant years for healthy development (Tooley, Bassett and Mackey, 2021)[26].

Tendency to be lazy

The view that we only use 10% of our brains is not true. It works together within a networked, integrated system of activity. However, it does have a tendency to be lazy, relying on instinct and intuition rather than logical, rational thinking (Boyd, 2008)[27].

Brain tissue has no pain receptors

Whilst it registers pain from all areas of the body, the brain does not feel pain itself (BrainLine, 2012)[28].

Neurons are information transmission superhighways

Information travels at different speeds within different types of neurons. Transmission speeds range from 1 to over 100 metres per second, and our brain produces enough electricity to power a light bulb (ScienceDaily, n.d.)[29].

In Summary

- The brain is 78% water; it accounts for 2% of our bodyweight; it uses 20% of our total resources of glucose and oxygen; it burns 20% to 30% of all the calories we consume.

- The brain uses energy from the food we eat and the air we breathe (glucose and oxygen) at a rate 10 times faster per unit mass than our muscles do (Padamsey and Rochefort, 2023)[30].

- As we mature, 50% of brain connections will be pared back as we shape and reshape neural networks through lack of use, overuse, or normal use (Lim et al., 2013)[31].

- Every time we focus attention on learning something new or change a behaviour, we activate a sequence of neural activity within the brain to create a new pathway via a process known as Hebb's law: cells that fire together, wire together.

- What we pay attention to shapes and reshapes the brain. By focusing attention and following a process of consistent practice, we restructure the brain and effect change.

- Whilst it is an effortful process, the ability of the brain to change provides the means for continual growth, change, and learning throughout life.

- There are many things that impact brain health; however, with small day-to-day changes, we support optimal brain functionality for improved performance and wellbeing.

"Whether you think you can, or you think you can't... you're right."

Henry Ford

Part Three

Mind

Introduction

It took me years to really understand the power of my own mind. Decades went past without me fully appreciating just how much my own thoughts were influencing my life. I hardly noticed what I was thinking most of the time. Apparently, this is not unusual: various studies suggest that we each have thousands of thoughts every day. If the thoughts are positive and supportive, there is no problem, but unfortunately, this is often not the case. It seems that many of the thoughts we experience – up to 80% – are more negative than positive, and an estimated 90% of them run on repeat (Rosenkranz et al., 2020)[1].

This is probably because the human system has an in-built negativity bias specifically designed to focus more on what is going wrong rather than what is going right around us. It is not a design fault. Without a finely tuned threat antenna, we would not have survived as a species. We needed to notice when predators were close or when we were being excluded from the tribe. If we missed these cues, it would have been a threat to our survival.

While the ramifications of missing such a threat cue may not be quite so severe in our modern world, the negativity bias remains just as active today as in the past. On average, it is said that we notice five times more threats in our environment than we do positive or rewarding things, and some in quarters, this ratio is stated as being up to nine times more.

It is crucial to understand and appreciate our negativity bias mechanism because, as is explored in the part on Brain, what we think not only shapes and reshapes the physical brain, it also directly impacts our physiology. Our thinking patterns influence pretty much everything we do and feel, from motivation to mood; from pain relief to performance.

If our thinking becomes stuck in a continuous negative loop, fuelled by gossip, toxic associates, or non-stop 'the world is collapsing' newsfeeds, it has a direct and often negative impact on us. This is perfectly illustrated by the placebo effect, where numerous studies all point to the undeniable fact that mind and body are intimately connected.

The Placebo Effect

The placebo effect is often referred to as the 'fake treatment': it is the sugar pill that replaces medical substances for research or drug testing purposes. Placebos still play a crucial role in medical science today, but it's unfortunate that the term 'fake treatment' has become so embedded in our collective understanding as it tends to downplay the power of the mind and our ability to harness it. Placebo studies have repeatedly demonstrated that the mind will influence the body, just as the body influences the mind, activating internal systems for healing and change.

In 2003, Fabrizio Benedetti, professor of physiology and neuroscience at the University of Turin, along with his colleagues, were curious to understand the impact of placebo on patients recovering from invasive surgery (Benedetti et al., 2003)[2]. Under normal circumstances following surgery, pain sets in once the anaesthesia wears off, and patients need pain relief in the form of morphine.

During the study, half the patients involved were given morphine manually by the doctor and the other half were treated for pain via intravenous therapy (IV drip) – but they were unaware that their IV drip treatment also contained morphine. When later reporting on felt pain versus pain relief, the group that had received morphine manually from the doctor reported a significant drop in felt pain compared to the IV group, even though both groups received the same dosage.

In 2007, Professors Alia Crum and Ellen Langer (Crum and Langer, 2007)[3] set out to discover if the placebo effect applied beyond medical situations, and they decided to test it in relation to physical change. They gathered 84 housekeepers from seven different hotels in the United States and interviewed them about their general health and fitness levels. Cleaning rooms and making beds is a highly physical activity, and yet two-thirds of those interviewed reported that they undertook no exercise at all, and when asked on a scale of 1 to 10 how much exercise they got, one-third said zero.

The housekeepers were measured for body weight, blood pressure, hip to waist ratio, and body mass index. Then they were split into two groups. Group one were asked to carry on as normal; nothing changed. However, group two were given a 15-minute presentation detailing all the muscle groups activated and calories burned during a housekeeper's daily work. Both groups were then asked to continue working as before for the next four-week period.

Four weeks later they were reassessed. The housekeepers in group one showed no change, whereas those in group two showed a decrease across all measured areas including an average weight loss of 2lbs and a reduction in systolic blood pressure of 10 points. The group two housekeepers did not report any increase in exercise outside of work, nor did they experience any increase in workload over the course of the study. In addition, they reported that their habits had not changed over the previous four weeks with respect to how much they ate (including servings of sugary foods and vegetables) or how much they drank (caffeine, alcohol, and water).

What is more fascinating is that Professor Crum's research did not stop there. How could she be sure that group one had not taken a sneaky visit to the gym or changed their eating habits during the four-week period? To address this question, she decided to measure the placebo impact on the hunger hormone known as ghrelin. Ghrelin is the hormone secreted in the gut that signals to the brain that we need to eat. For many years, scientists believed ghrelin only responded to the nutrients it met in the stomach. When we eat a big meal, ghrelin levels go down, signalling that we've eaten enough, whereas with small snacks, ghrelin levels drop but not to the same extent.

In 2011, Crum recruited a group of participants and paid them $75 dollars each to drink a milkshake on two separate occasions (Crum et al., 2011)[4]; the only caveat was that during the process, nurses were to take intravenous blood samples at predetermined time points to measure ghrelin levels. During the first visit, participants were given a Sensi-shake containing 0% fat, 0% sugar, and 140 calories.

The shake was not high in calories and while ghrelin levels dropped, they did not drop by much. The second time, participants were asked to drink an Indulgence shake which comprised 30g of fat, 56g of sugar, and 620 calories. This time, ghrelin levels dropped significantly – in fact three times more than before.

What was interesting about this study was that in reality, both shakes were the same: each milkshake contained 380 calories. The only thing that changed was the belief the participants had regarding what they were drinking. At the time, this research was considered groundbreaking, with the scientific community accepting that mindset as well as nutrients determine the ghrelin response.

These and many more studies like them continually reinforce the mind-body connection and how the mind can and does impact our internal state in a myriad of different ways. To bring this to life for yourself, try the following exercise. It takes two to three minutes, and it perfectly demonstrates how the mind can shift how we feel. Read through the instructions, ensure you are in a safe space, and give it a go.

Tired or Energised Exercise

Part One

- Use a phone or find a watch that gives an alarm when a minute has passed.

- First, make yourself comfortable in a seated position, ensuring that you can safely stand or move in your chair when required.

- On pressing the timer, think deeply about how tired you are. You have been busy; it has been a long day/night and you need to rest. Think it out, imagine the tiredness in your limbs and the heaviness of your eyes.

- Remain in this state for the full minute.

- When the timer goes off, stand up and shake yourself out – make sure it is safe to stand without a trip or fall.

- If you are unable to stand, shake yourself out in the seated position.

- Get comfortable in your seat once more.

Part Two

- Reset the timer.

- On pressing the timer, think deeply about how energised you are. You have so much energy you don't know what to do with it. You want to move, run, dance. You are eager to get into action; again, think it out, imagine the energy running through your veins and how your limbs want to move.

- Remain in this state for the full minute.
- When the timer goes off, stand up and shake yourself out – again make sure it is safe to stand without a trip or fall.
- If you are unable to stand, shake yourself out in the seated position.
- Get comfortable in your seat once more.

Part Three

- What did you notice?
- What was the difference between the first minute and the second minute?
- Were there any changes in how you felt?
- Were there any differences in the sensations you experienced or in the way you stood up/moved around your chair?

The tired or energised exercise is a relatively simple activity designed to demonstrate how thought can change our internal state. However, it's worth remembering that the placebo effect is a complex combination of internal conscious, subconscious, and unconscious processing. The mind uses conscious thought to think, and it is also informed by the more deeply embedded beliefs, some of which exist outside conscious awareness, and by the rituals or triggers we are exposed to.

Sometimes there is a continuing battle between the different modes of processing. For example, I can consciously tell myself I am great at my job, yet also lie awake at 3am, paralysed with fear, rooted in strongly entrenched beliefs about my inability to do that exact same job. Alternatively, I can be told I'm an outstanding presenter, yet every time I enter a meeting, my fear of being judged sends my anxiety into overdrive. It is therefore helpful to understand the interplay between our thinking processes or, more simply, the way the brain thinks.

Thinking Processes

Through the work of Nobel Prize-winning economist and psychologist Daniel Kahneman (Kahneman, 2011)[5], we have learned much about how the brain thinks and makes decisions. He identified that the brain thinks in two different ways, describing the two systems as System 1, the intuitive, automatic fast route; and System 2, the slower, more analytical route.

We should note here that other researchers have raised concerns that the System 1 and System 2 terminology may be oversimplistic. After all, the brain is complex and many interconnected regions of the brain and sets of systems are active when engaging in conscious, subconscious and/ or unconscious processing. Acknowledging this, the main takeaway here is that the brain undertakes mental work in two different ways. System 1 is fast, automatic, and operates largely outside conscious awareness, and System 2 is slow, considered, and associated with conscious thought.

Personally, I've found it easier to remember what the two systems do by colour coding into Blue and Yellow. In the following image, Blue represents Kahneman's System 1 and Yellow represents System 2. I'm sure neuroscientists will faint at the oversimplification; however, the Blue/Yellow distinction has been well-received over the years with high memory recall, making it much easier to remember the brain's thinking systems and the impact this has on what we do and how we behave.

The Blue/Yellow Brain

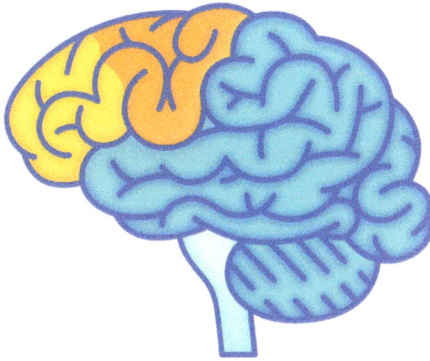

The Yellow Brain

The area shown in yellow sits just behind the forehead as a section of the frontal cortex (shown in yellow plus orange), the evolutionary, newer part of the brain. We discuss the yellow area in the part on Brain, referring to it by its formal name, the prefrontal cortex or the executive centre. Slow, controlled, deliberate, and intentional: it's the area credited with making us human; it's involved in regulating behaviour, governing social control, and housing active working memory. It allows us to set objectives, to think logically, to plan, and to strategise.

You might think that when we are awake, we spend most of our time in the Yellow brain. In reality, this is not true. We actually only use Yellow brain resources an estimated 3% to 5% of the time. For the rest of the time, we function in the Blue, relying on habits, mental shortcuts, and automatic processing, which have been laid down over a lifetime.

Why is this? Well, the Yellow brain literally eats up internal resources to work. It drains energy in the form of glucose and oxygen, making us tired and hungry. Remember, the brain's main objective is to keep us safe and well. It will never allow all its internal resources to be used up unnecessarily. For this reason, it will always call on the less energy hungry Blue brain whenever it can. Consequently, the brain manages our internal resources with military precision, only using precious energy when absolutely necessary. This makes certain that there are always energy reserves available to get the human system out of danger, if and when needed, at a moment's notice.

Still not sure?

At speed, answer the following questions.

1. What is $1 + 1$?

2. What is $2 + 2$?

3. What is $346 \div 7.5$?

Did you notice how your stomach knotted or your brain went, "Do we really have to?" when you reached question 3? This is because to answer question 3, unless we are a mathematical genius, we must stop and consciously think, which drains precious internal energy to engage the Yellow brain and effortfully work out the answer. Whereas, the responses to questions 1 and 2 come to mind automatically, easily, and without conscious effort, located as they are within the Blue brain.

Whenever and wherever it can, the brain will avoid using Yellow brain resources. There is an exception to this, which is when we move into a state of flow. Flow is when we are so focused on an activity that everything else seems to disappear. We are fully engaged and lose track of time because we are enjoying what we're doing. It feels effortless, like we're in the zone, and we perform at our best. Whether it's playing a musical instrument, engaging in a sport, or working on a project, flow is when we're completely absorbed and feel a deep sense of satisfaction.

The Flow State

According to psychologist Mihaly Csikszentmihalyi, who wrote the book *Flow* (Csikszentmihalyi, 1990)[6], the only time our Yellow brain is functioning in an effortless way is when we are in a state of flow: when our strengths are matched by the challenge or challenges we face, so much so that maintaining focused attention requires no exertion, leaving the Yellow brain free to focus on the task in hand. This is when we are at our most brilliant, even though such experiences may not necessarily be pleasant at the time they occur. A runner may be exhausted with aching limbs and a throbbing head at the end of a marathon, yet they will still feel exhilarated from the experience.

Flow is often associated with peak performance – when we are at our most productive and efficient. Top athletes, writers, or musicians are often given as examples of bringing flow to life because the very nature of what they do and how they do it means that they are continually working towards peak experience. They have rules within which to learn new skills. They set up goals, solicit ongoing feedback, and continually push themselves to achieve higher levels of performance, one step, one challenge after another.

This ongoing personal growth sits at the heart of flow and with the application of similar rules, it is possible for all of us to experience states of flow, thereby improving our own day-to-day experiences. The more we experience flow, the stronger, more confident, and more creative we feel.

Research has shown that despite many of us agreeing that work is an imposition and something we would rather avoid, we undergo more flow experiences at work than we do during our leisure time (Stefan E., 2014)[7]. This is particularly true if our leisure time is relatively unchallenging, such as watching television, chatting to friends, or going out to dinner. Increased flow moments are achieved through enhanced personal discipline. They demand that we clarify what we want to focus on and set clear, challenging – yet attainable – goals to guide us, that we continue to solicit training and support, and actively seek feedback on progress made.

As Mihaly explains, if challenges are too easy, we get back to flow by increasing their intensity, and if challenges are too great, we return to flow by learning the skills necessary for the challenge faced. Flow is a form of self-discipline: the ability to control our attention and apply disciplined concentration to the task in front of us, stretching skills and capabilities in whatever it is we have chosen to focus on.

The relationship between flow states and the activation of the Yellow brain can vary among individuals and across different activities. For some, it could be creating a beautiful garden; for others, it could be rock climbing, preparing for a presentation, or drafting an important report. While the task doesn't matter for flow to manifest, a flow state is never guaranteed. However, it becomes much more likely if we:

- identify a task that is challenging but not overwhelming.
- allocate dedicated time with clear start and end times.
- set precise goals to ensure we are clear on what we want to achieve.
- focus attention – switch off the phone and eliminate all distractions.
- continually work to develop our skills, practising regularly, and striving for mastery.
- seek feedback, monitor progress, and make adjustments as necessary.
- look after ourselves properly, enhancing our ability to enter and sustain the flow state.

Before moving on, you may want to reflect how often you enter a state of flow and what you might consider doing to increase the number of flow experiences you have.

The Blue Brain

This brain area is hardwired, dominant, and associated with the evolutionary older brain. The Blue brain is primarily responsible for the survival and safety of the human system, and it works largely outside conscious awareness. It is spontaneous and typically reactionary, taking information from the senses and long-term memory or habit stores to direct what we do and how we react, continually generating story from the words, feelings, and actions it experiences.

With its instantaneous speed, driven by instinct and prior learning, the Blue brain acts as a 24-hour rapid response system, one with little understanding of either logic or statistics. It works quickly, drawing on available energy and connects all parts of the brain in a pattern of cognitive, emotional, and physical responses as it reacts to the signals and senses from both the inner and outer world. Importantly, and unlike the Yellow brain, it requires limited energy to function and can make sense of different situations within milliseconds.

If we are in danger, we don't need to think and ponder on a solution – we just need to do something. If we are faced with an aggressive dog, there is no time to engage the slower Yellow brain to think it out. We just need to react quickly and run. The ability to respond automatically and 'just run' is a function of the Blue brain. It has enormous capacity: metaphorically speaking, it is the equivalent of the milky way compared to the tiny cubic square metre of capacity available via the Yellow brain.

Most of our everyday reactions, impressions, and decisions are driven by the Blue brain, and even when we believe we're making decisions based on our rational Yellow self, the Blue brain, with its mix of beliefs, biases, and intuition drives many of our choices. Often described as the 'stranger within,' we need Blue brain functionality precisely because of its instinctive and fast nature along with its ability to react instantaneously, keeping us safe when needed.

Yin and Yang

The Blue and Yellow brain areas each have their own personalities, abilities, and limitations, always working together in concert through a coherent web of neural and chemical connections. When in balance and healthy, their operation is seamless, especially as we switch between different ways of thinking in a fluid response to both internal and external stimuli. However, when these brain areas are out of balance with each other, the implications can be devastating and far-reaching. This is particularly the case when we push ourselves to keep going despite depleted resources.

Remember, the brain's main function is to keep the human system safe and well. When it registers that resources are depleted or it perceives the human system to be under threat due to hunger, tiredness and/or chronic stress, it will work to conserve energy and oxygen, ready for fight, flight, or freeze.

'The brain's main function is to keep the human system safe and well.'

As the Yellow brain uses a lot of energy to function, one of the brain's first actions will be to more or less switch the Yellow brain off and rely on the Blue brain to keep us going because it drains less energy. In fact, when we are stressed, tired, hungry, or fearful, that cubic square metre of Yellow brain capacity and/or functionality is reduced to the equivalent of a cubic square centimetre! We may manage to keep going but not without suffering the consequences including:

- an inability to think analytically and logically (much needed in our knowledge-working world)

- an inability to moderate behaviour (important to maintain great relationships)

- an inability to facilitate personal change (we need the Yellow brain to focus attention)

- an inability to challenge intrusive thoughts (rumination goes into overdrive)

Chronic stress has a particularly negative impact, resulting in the almost total loss of rational Yellow brain thinking. It's reported that IQ drops by up to 13% (UPI, 1983)[8] when functioning under chronic stress conditions, the equivalent of reducing normal intelligence to that of a person with learning difficulties. We become hypersensitive and emotional; we lack good judgment, relying more on gut instinct to make sense of what is happening. We fall back on unconscious bias, which runs much closer to the surface when the Yellow brain is not functioning well.

Our ability to think rationally and consciously deteriorates, along with our ability to challenge negative thought patterns and damaging rumination loops. The Blue brain increasingly drives our thoughts, guided by out-of-date beliefs and stories buried deep within the brain's memory banks. Increased feelings of imposter syndrome are shown to correlate with chronic stress and burnout. When those, "I am a fraud," thoughts emerge from deep within the Blue brain, we are unable to quieten or challenge the internal noise when the Yellow brain is not engaged.

We should always remind ourselves that our thoughts are not always logical and certainly not always accurate, that the more tired, depleted, or stressed we are, the more likely it is that our Blue brain will be spinning us an unhelpful yarn based on out-of-date data. Just because we think something does not make it true.

To maintain a healthy Yin and Yang between the Yellow and Blue brain, it is essential to take care of the basics. A balance of sleep, food, rest, and exercise is necessary. We also need to feel safe and to live and work within an environment where we feel included and where we belong. Exclusion, isolation, and lack of safety all have a direct negative impact on Yellow brain functionality. It's important to recognise this, to engage in activities that support good brain health generally and also to practise techniques that help us moderate those automatic negative thought patterns and break those damaging rumination loops when they arise.

Managing Negative Thoughts

Just as we all have negative thoughts, we can all get better at shutting them down. It's a matter of awareness, time, and practice. The effort is worth it because years of torment by out-of-date, inaccurate thoughts is no fun for anyone. Dr Daniel Amen, in his book *Change Your Brain, Change Your Life* (Amen, 2016)[9], identified nine Automatic Negative Thoughts or ANTs for short (see table). He invites us to recognise them for what

Automatic Negative Thoughts The nine varieties of ANT (Amen, 2016)
1. 'All or Nothing' thinking: thoughts that things are all good or all bad; there is nothing in-between.
2. 'Always' thinking: thinking in words like always, never, no one, everyone, every time or everything. Believing something will always repeat itself. ("No one ever calls me." / "You never listen to me.")
3. Focusing on the Negative: only seeing the bad in a situation, ignoring any of the good that might happen. There is always a positive – look for it and focus on it.
4. Fortune Telling: predicting the worst possible outcome to a situation with little or no evidence for it.
5. Mind Reading: believing that you know what another person is thinking even though they have not told you. ("Those people are mad at me; they don't like me; they are talking about me; they will think I am stupid.")
6. Thinking with your Feelings: believing negative feelings without ever questioning them ("I feel stupid; I feel like a failure."). Whenever there is a strong negative feeling, check it out and don't just believe it.
7. Guilt Beatings: thinking in words like should, must, ought, or have to. As human beings, whenever we feel we 'must' do something, no matter what it is, don't want to do it. (Instead of, "I ought to call my mother," think of it in terms of, "I want to call my mother.")
8. Labelling: attaching a negative label to ourselves or someone else inhibits our ability to take a clear look at the situation (jerk, idiot, spoiled brat). Negative labels are harmful and stop us dealing with ourselves or others in a reasonable way.
9. Blaming (King RED): blaming someone else for the problems we have. Whenever we blame someone or something else for the problems in our life, we become powerless to change anything. Stay away from blaming, shaming and/or complaining and take personal responsibility for addressing the problems you have.

they are, questioning their validity rather than listening to and accepting them as accurate facts. He considered the red ANTs (shown in bold) to be the most damaging.

An effective way to identify whether you are prone to ANTs, or more general unhelpful thought patterns, is to try and notice when you have them and write them down as they arise. The more detail you can recall around what happens when you have such thoughts, the more likely you are to recognise that thought in the future. It's a process of catch it, check it, change it:

- catch it by becoming aware of when the thought appears – notice the triggers.
- check it by questioning the validity – is it really true?
- change it through the use of different techniques – such as reframing (viewing a situation from a different perspective).

In addition, as you begin to understand the short-, mid- and longer-term impacts, the more committed you become to creating alternative thought patterns. Use the Unhelpful Thoughts Framework provided on the following page, adopted, and adapted from Schwartz and Gladding (2012)[10], to guide your thinking and to catch some of the thoughts that are stopping you and/or getting in your way.

Having worked through the framework and identified any unhelpful thoughts, take a moment to check the validity of the thought/s. Reflect on the following sequence of questions, adopted and adapted from the work of Byron Katie (Katie and Mitchell, 2017)[11]. If possible, work with your

The Unhelpful Thoughts Framework

Name the unhelpful thought	Describe any accompanying uncomfortable sensations	Capture identified impacts (short, medium and/or long-term)	Consider the thought: Is it true or false?
Example: I'm not as good as everyone else, so I won't apply for the promotion.	**Example:** I feel blocked, upset and frustrated every time a promotion comes along.	**Example:** I curtail my own development and career progression and miss out on the financial benefits.	**True:** What if anything can I do about it? **False:** Close it down.

notebook rather than thinking it out in the mind. The process of writing forces us to organise our thoughts, making them clearer and more structured. As we write, we crystallise our often-nebulous thoughts into tangible words and sentences, which can lead to a deeper level of understanding.

1. Is the unhelpful thought 100% true?

2. Are you 100% sure it is true?

3. Who says it is true? Is there evidence or is it an opinion?

    a. If the thought is understood to be 100% true, sit quietly and take a moment to brainstorm all the things you could do to change the situation. If enhanced skills are required to achieve the desired promotion, you might sign up for further training, engage a coach, or solicit feedback to identify specific areas of development. This activity moves us into 'change it' action planning, engaging Yellow brain resources, and shifting the negative thought into a more positive, action-orientated way of thinking.

    b. When you have brainstormed all you can, put your notes aside and carry on with your day. Only come back to your notes a few hours later or even the next day. This allows the brain to keep working on ideas in the background so that when you do pick up your notes again, you will have some additions to the list that you had not considered previously, plus any emerging ideas on how to get started. The brain works for us, even when we are not aware of it!

If after having answered questions 1, 2, and 3 there is a realisation that the thought is not true yet the job of changing it and reducing its power is proving hard to do, work through the next sequence of questions. As before, aim to follow the process of writing out the answers rather than working them through in your mind.

4. What does holding onto this thought actually do for you?

5. Who will you become 10 years from now if you keep holding onto this thought?

6. What will the cost be 10 years from now if this thought is not changed?

7. Who would you become and how would you act/what would you do if this thought did not exist?

Now consider and respond to the following:

- What do you want to think instead?
- What opportunities might open with this new thought?
- What actions might you take with this new thought?
- What can you do now? What steps can you take to turn this new thought into reality?
- How does it feel to be free from the old thought?

Take a moment to reflect on your answers and feel the release of the thought that was holding you back. You might find it helpful to write the old thought on a piece of paper: take a breath, feel the release, and then rip up or scrunch the paper before actively throwing it away – the physical act of throwing it away is a release in itself. If you are working with a very deep-seated belief, you may need to work through the process more than once.

An alternative or an addition to the above framework is learning the art of ABC. This is a 'change it' exercise that takes no more than two to three minutes and can be practised anywhere.

The Art of ABC

If you find yourself thinking an uncomfortable negative thought, learn to make a shift with ABC. The art of choosing may feel uncomfortable at first, particularly if those unhelpful thought patterns have been around for a long time. This is not unusual. Change, as we know from neuroplasticity in the part on Brain, takes practice.

We all have the power to choose what we think; however, it is also true to say that this is practically impossible if the Yellow brain is offline. The ABC method, developed by Clare Josa (Josa, 2020)[12], is a simple yet effective way of navigating past unhelpful thoughts emerging in the mind, regardless of where we are or what we are doing. Work with one of the thoughts identified, or choose another one, and follow the ABC process outlined here.

A – Accept: Accept the thought, name it, but don't engage with it. Think of it as a cloud floating past overhead and nothing more. When a thought is accepted without judgment, it loses all its power. Remember, it is not the thought itself that causes us harm; it is the story we wrap around it that then builds out into an emotional animal that we find difficult to control.

B – Breathe: Use breath to prevent the nervous system activating in response to the thought. Using the diaphragm, inhale deeply and focus on expanding the belly outwards, then slowly exhale, drawing the belly back in towards the spine. Repeat the exercise four times. This resets the nervous system and creates a space to choose a different thought path. Unhelpful thoughts will automatically prime the nervous system to activate the stress response, reducing our ability to think logically via the Yellow brain pathways.

C – Choose: Consciously choose to think a different, more productive, helpful thought. It could be something you are grateful for or a thought that gives a sense of happiness and calm. If you get stuck, ask yourself, in the context of what you were previously thinking about, "What do I want to do or think instead?" Let the new thought shift from thinking to feeling in the body.

Ensure the new thought is positively framed. The mind finds it very difficult to process words such as "don't", "not", "stop," etc. For example, "I don't want to suffer from nerves when leading a meeting," means we must first recall the nerves, which takes us back into the stress response and the unhelpful thought process. The "don't" gets lost in the process and we end up reinforcing the unhelpful thought. It's much better to change it to, "When leading a meeting, I am calm, confident, and know my subject."

Embedded ways of thinking take time to shift, but with practice, the ABC process becomes faster and more fluid. To accelerate the process, or even as a stand-alone, you can also consider engaging in gratitude practice. This is a highly effective tool for regulating emotion, reducing stress, and creating positive moods, supporting a focus on the positive aspects of life whilst contributing to greater long-term resilience.

Gratitude Practice

Practising gratitude is where we take a moment each day to focus our attention on things that make us happy: a beautiful sunny day, food on the table, or the love of a significant person. It can be a purely mental process where we simply reflect on what we are grateful for or a more physical process, with gratitude moments captured at the end of each day or week in a gratitude journal.

In an experimental comparison in 2003, researchers Robert Emmons and Michael McCullough (Emmons, R. A., & McCullough, M. E., 2003)[13] discovered that people who practised gratitude and/or kept a gratitude journal on a weekly basis exercised more regularly, reported fewer negative physical symptoms, felt better about their lives, and were generally 25% happier. A related benefit of practising gratitude was observed in personal goal attainment. Participants who kept gratitude lists were more likely to have made progress toward important personal goals (academic, interpersonal, and health-based) over a two-month period, compared to subjects in other experimental conditions.

Take a moment and use the form below to stop and consider what you are grateful for. Be as specific as you can. For example, you may be grateful for your family; however, consider the detail of exactly what this means for you. If the statements are too general, they lose their power. Aim to do this at least once a day for 30 days. At the end of 30 days, reflect on any changes you may have noticed in terms of outlook, positivity, mood, or anything else.

Practising Gratitude
1.
2.
3.
4.
5.

Practising Receiving Gratitude

In 2017, a study by researcher Professor Sara Algoe (The University of North Carolina at Chapel Hill, n.d.)[14] highlighted that in addition to practising gratitude, receiving thanks or gratitude also has a powerful impact. This is particularly so when the thanks or gratitude is embedded in story.

Stories shift the physiology of the listener; we experience a deepening sense of gratitude when we recall a time when we or another felt a deep sense of gratitude for something that happened to us or them. Maybe we were given a hand when we needed it, someone remembered our birthday, or a colleague thanked us for a job well done. The more we recall the story, the more gratitude we experience.

Whilst receiving is powerful, we can't determine when someone articulates their gratitude for something we have done. However, we can capture the story of when this happened to us and bring it to mind on a regular basis. The more we do this, the more we experience a genuine chemical and neural activation uplift. The best way to capture gratitude that we have received is to write it in a diary or preserve it in a digital document. The following structure is helpful for capturing and revisiting received gratitude.

Capturing Gratitude

Identify when you or another person received gratitude from someone else. Create a meaningful story: make notes and recount details in simple bullet points for easy ongoing recall. The story can be yours personally or another person's story – the impact is the same.

Capture the essence of:

- What happened – what did you or the other person do? Why, what, when, how? Express any thoughts about the excitement or joy including any struggle or tension that was overcome.

- Describe how the experience of receiving gratitude impacted you or another person. How was it delivered? What did you feel? How did you respond?

Revisiting Received Gratitude

Before reading your received gratitude stories, take a moment to relax and calm the mind. Take three deep breaths, using the diaphragm, with long exhales to ensure you are in the best state possible to absorb and celebrate the received gratitude. Then follow the steps outlined:

- Read one of the captured stories.

- Feel into it, experiencing sensations, feelings, and emotions of gratitude in the body.

- Practice for a minimum of 60 seconds and up to 5 minutes – aim to do this three times per week or as needed.

- If time allows, make a note in your gratitude journal of your state before and after the practice. This further embeds the feeling of uplift from the practice into memory.

Don't underestimate the importance of cultivating the act of expressing and exchanging gratitude. The more it becomes a genuine day-to-day habit, the more we benefit from its impact and the more we positively affect and influence those around us. Quite simply, the more we give, the more comes back.

It's important to remember that gratitude should always be grounded in truth. It is impossible to lie to ourselves or others whilst also maintaining the benefits of gratitude practice. For example, we may be having a really bad day, and while we can't pretend to be grateful for a bad day, we can still be grateful for the smile someone gave us when we walked in through the door or the thank-you note someone sent for a job well done.

Rumination and Rumination Hacks

The more we fixate on the negative aspects of certain situations, activities, or people, the more likely we are to develop an unhealthy habit of continual rumination. Although we can be grateful for the magic of the brain's changeability, it does also mean we can easily embed negative neural pathways in the brain that set a pattern of unhelpful rumination.

Remember, the brain has no moral code; it will rewire itself in response to where we focus attention. Unlike self-reflection, rumination magnifies the severity of problems, making it harder to find a productive way out of a particular situation. It can feel like a woodpecker continually pecking away at us, activating the stress response, depleting energy, draining thinking resources, and often causing fitful, disturbed sleep.

I've found there is no one thing that alleviates rumination. It requires conscious effort and is more a process of test and learn while we work to disrupt the cycle and redirect focus. That said, disrupting rumination is essential for wellbeing and the more we work to disrupt the cycle, the less invasive and the easier the process becomes.

There are many different approaches, some of which are highlighted here. I invite you to experiment with different strategies to find the ones that really work for you. Don't beat yourself up if you can't refocus your attention first time round, and don't allow frustration to cause you to give up. Deeply embedded negative rumination patterns take time to shift; they cling on when challenged. It takes patience, a big dose of self-love, and consistent work over time to establish more positive and joyful thought patterns.

Mindfulness

By learning how to focus our attention and redirect our thoughts, we can improve our mental and emotional abilities. When we shift our attention from the past or future to the present moment, we give ourselves a chance to change how we feel. The more we focus on what is happening right now, the better we can control our emotions when we are triggered. Mindfulness involves noticing and observing uncomfortable feelings and thoughts without getting caught up in them. As we get better at this, negative patterns of thinking become less intense and occur less frequently.

However, we can find sitting with our thoughts very difficult. When psychologist Professor Timothy Wilson (University of Virginia) and his colleagues asked participants to sit alone with their thoughts for a period of about 10 minutes, most of the subjects were miserable (Wilson et al., 2014)[15]. Some chose the option of giving themselves a mild electric shock rather than simply sitting there and being present. As Wilson stated, "The untutored mind does not like to be alone with itself."

As a personal example, I found sitting quietly with my thoughts almost impossible to begin with. Even two minutes was a challenge. My mind insisted I had better things to do, so much so it created such an internal conflict that I felt physically sick, and I was forced to stop by my own system. It took four to five months of regular practice for me to work up to a comfortable 20 minutes. I am pleased to report that I can now comfortably do an hour, reaping the benefits of this quiet, reflective time.

If you find sitting quietly really does not work for you, start by finding mindful moments during the day. A gateway to becoming more mindful is noticing how we experience our food: the taste, colour, and smell. We can also be mindful of the scenery as we walk to work or look out of the window. The essence of mindfulness is the ability to focus attention on the present moment, observing thoughts without judgment. This can be practised anywhere, building up to longer, deeper exercises as our mental and emotional capabilities strengthen.

Grounding

Grounding is similar to mindfulness in that it helps us reconnect with the present moment, especially when experiencing anxiety, panic attacks, or the sensation of overwhelm. By engaging in physical, mental, or soothing grounding practices, we bring our attention back to the present, disrupting the rumination pattern, and restoring mental balance. We can practise grounding in a few different ways:

- **Physical Grounding** involves harnessing bodily sensations to anchor ourselves in the present. Techniques for this include deep breathing practices, carrying a small object with a distinct texture that can be touched, or simply pushing our feet firmly into the floor to feel the connection with the ground.

- **Mental Grounding** uses mental exercises to divert the mind, which could be counting, reciting something, or engaging in memory exercises.

- **Soothing Grounding** focuses more on comforting actions, such as listening to peaceful music or visualising a calm, happy place.

Regardless of which practice you prefer, the act of grounding helps us to stabilise our mental state by shifting our attention from our internal turmoil to something we can do or think about that is taking place in the present moment.

Emotional Journalling

Emotional Journalling is a highly effective tool for both emotional regulation and stress relief, allowing us to externalise and discard negative thoughts that endlessly roll around the mind. As thoughts leave the mind, we introduce distance, which often brings a greater level of clarity. This process enables us to process rising emotion better; it stalls the negative loop and provides a space for more constructive reflection and solutions.

Professor James Pennebaker from the University of Texas spent years researching the links between writing and emotional processing (Pennebaker, 2017)[16]. He invited participants to write about emotionally charged episodes for 20 minutes each day over a period of three days only, discarding the writings at the end of each session. His findings showed that participants experienced a marked increase in their physical and mental wellbeing; not only did they report being happier, less depressed, and less anxious, they also experienced lower blood pressure, greater immune function, and made fewer visits to the doctor, even in the months after the writing sessions had taken place.

Pennebaker also ran an experiment with 100 senior engineers who were laid off from a Dallas computer company. Most of the participants were over the age of 50. They had all worked at that company for their entire professional lives, and four months after the layoffs, they had not found another job. The group was divided into two. The first group was asked to journal how being laid off made them feel as well as any impact on health, marriage, finances, and the future. The second group were not asked to write anything about their experience.

Initially, there was no difference recorded between the two groups in terms of motivation or the effort that they were making to find a new job. However, within a few short months of the activity beginning, the journalling group were three times more likely to have been re-employed than the non-journalling group.

A note of caution – the purpose of emotional journalling is not repeating and ruminating on the negativity over and over again over extended periods of time, which is both unhelpful and destructive. There is a difference between keeping a diary or a journal of life events and the emotional journalling referenced here. The writings for this exercise are time-bound and thrown away once the writing sessions are complete. The purpose of this process is to externalise and discard, not to write as a memory jog for ongoing rumination.

Physical Activity

As we know, physical activity has many benefits. One of the more important ones, as far as rumination is concerned, is that it takes us out of the mind. When we get into the body and move, we shift attention away from our thoughts, breaking the ruminative cycle. It is argued that the more aerobic the activity, the more impactful the result – and this makes sense.

Engaging in higher aerobic exercise offers a multitude of benefits (Netz, Y. 2017)[17]. Not only does it release feel-good neurotransmitters like endorphins, dopamine, and serotonin, but it also requires focused attention, effectively diverting us from negative thought patterns and rumination. Furthermore, exercise reduces levels of cortisol, the stress hormone, thereby contributing to lower anxiety and reduced rumination.

Regular aerobic exercise also enhances cognitive function, equipping us to better regulate our thoughts and emotions, ultimately reducing the tendency for rumination. These combined physiological and psychological effects create a powerful mechanism for breaking free from the cycle of rumination and promoting overall mental wellbeing.

I want to emphasise that we don't need to go for a run or head to the gym if that does not suit us. We can engage in vigorous outdoor activity such as gardening, jumping on the bike, or even doing a house or room clean. The more we move, the more we break the rumination loop.

Savouring

Savouring is the ability to extend and savour positive experiences. All too often, we rush past the good things that happen to us and don't enjoy the full benefit of those experiences. As we learn how to hold onto and savour those moments, we not only increase the immediate intensity of the feeling, but we also create a much longer-lasting stream of positive thoughts and emotions.

Several studies have shown that when we stop to savour a pleasant event or experience, we benefit from a happiness boost (Villani et al., 2023)[18]. Interestingly, this is not limited to the present moment: we can savour what is happening now, what happened in the past, or what might come to pass in the future. We can also appreciate and savour someone else's pleasure. Taking time to savour a positive experience helps to strengthen the neural pathways to long-term memory, making it easier to recall that positive experience in the future.

As we can see from the examples given here, there are different ways to interrupt rumination patterns. They don't all work for everyone and finding the best option is an ongoing process of testing and learning. It takes time and can be a frustrating process; however, it is worth it. Those negative thought patterns get in the way of a wonderful life, not to mention that they are often inaccurate and out-of-date, creating ways of thinking and behaving that hold us back.

So play with it. Find what works for you, and take it one day at a time. It is only when we look back with the passage of time that we are able to see just how far we have come. At its core, rumination is just a habit, and all habits can be changed thanks to the brain's natural changeability. Don't live with it: get into action and rewire to the positive.

Note: If the rumination habit is severely impacting the quality of your life, don't hesitate to speak with a health professional, a cognitive behavioural therapy (CBT) specialist, or similar for more tailored support to suit your needs.

In Summary

- Our thinking patterns influence pretty much everything we do and feel from motivation to mood and from pain relief to performance.

- Placebo studies have repeatedly demonstrated that the mind acts on the body, activating internal systems for healing and change.

- The brain undertakes mental work along two pathways: the Blue brain, which is fast, automatic, and operates largely outside conscious awareness, and the Yellow brain, which is slow, considered, and associated with conscious thought.

- The Yellow brain (System 2), sits just behind the forehead and is the area that makes humans unique. It tires easily, uses a lot of energy through glucose and oxygen, and it is sensitive to the neurochemical environment that exist within the brain.

- The only time the Yellow thinking system functions in a non-effortful way is when we are in a state of flow.

- The Blue brain (System 1), is hardwired, dominant, and associated with the older, evolutionary brain. It is primarily responsible for our survival and safety.

- The Blue brain operates largely outside conscious awareness, and it reacts to the signals and senses from our inner and outer world.

- When we are tired or stressed, when our Blue brain is overpowering and in control, we become hypersensitive and emotional, often behaving with poor judgment, thus making it difficult to challenge negative thought patterns.

"Take care of your body. it's the only place you have to live."

Jim Rohn

Part Four

Body

Introduction

I love this quote from Jim Rohn. It always serves as a reminder that without this body of mine, I really do cease to exist. After all, the body is the container through which we experience the world and how the world experiences us. Information flows through the five senses – sight, smell, touch, hearing, and taste – continuously updating us with information regarding our external surroundings, while our physicality enables us to navigate fluidly through and around our surroundings.

I also like to think about it in this way: the skull protects the brain, emotion flows through the body, which influences our responses, and then that same body generates gestures and expressions for all manner of non-verbal communication with others. Occasionally, the body may break. We may have to lose or remove parts of it and sometimes certain elements just don't function quite as they are supposed to. However, wherever possible, this wonderful body of ours will always work hard to repair itself or make up for what it has lost.

All bodies are different, coming in a variety of shapes and sizes and all beautiful in their own way. This part on

Body is not about reshaping ourselves to match the mostly unattainable looks and forms of those we may see on social media (who, by the way, have airbrushed themselves into fantasy land). Neither is it about signing up for the next Iron Man competition – although feel free to do so if that floats your boat! Rather, it's about understanding that our body is not static: it is alive and constantly in motion. It has its own language and way of communicating, and the more we work with it, listen, and respond to its needs, the healthier and happier we are.

Understand Your Body's Language

Just as the quality of a new suit is dependent on the value of the raw materials used to make it, the ability of the body to repair itself is dependent on the quality of the cells it produces: for example, how easily the skin repairs itself following injury or the liver's ability to restore itself if damaged. The quality of those cells relies on inputs such as the food we eat, the water we drink, and the exercise we undertake.

Nutritious food provides the raw materials the body needs to create high-quality proteins, which are the molecular building blocks of cells. Whereas poor quality food, as highlighted in *Mind Over Matter* by Dr Dawson Church (Church and Dispenza, 2019)[1], means the body must work with substandard materials, resulting in trade-offs and compromises that ultimately damage our health.

Over the years, I have got much better at listening to my body, understanding its language, and what it is trying to tell me. For those of us prepared to listen, our body has ways of advising us when things are out of balance: pain in the shoulders may indicate too long hunched over a laptop; the continuous coughs and colds are perhaps a sign of a low immune system in desperate need of rest and recovery; the continual pull to devour high-sugar, fatty foods during the day is possibly a demand to replace lost energy from poor sleep habits.

The body is constantly changing as it responds to thoughts, social life, and daily activity. Everything we do has a consequence. Our physiology dictates mood, with a low mood serving as a good indication that the body is out of balance. A simple example of how depleted energy within the body can impact mood is the speed with which we can move to anger when we are hungry.

Thankfully, there are many small practices we can incorporate into day-to-day life to balance the body better, some of which we have already been introduced to. The basics of food, exercise, sleep, managing negative thoughts, and having regular rest are essential. However, don't underestimate the power of interventions such as gratitude, which is a powerful body booster. As we see in the part on Mind, the practice of gratitude is known to contribute to a reduction in stress, which consumes a significant amount of the body's energy, as well as supporting the release of dopamine, helping optimise our body's use of energy.

There is also a growing body of evidence that indicates people who volunteer and give their time to others are often rewarded with better physical health, including lower blood pressure and a longer lifespan. Then there is the management of personal boundaries, which are invaluable for setting clear expectations, defining what is OK and not OK for us, and ultimately providing a framework for conserving personal energy levels.

Manage Body Energy

It's helpful to think of body energy levels as we would a bank account: if we slip into the red, there are consequences and fees to be paid. Take some time to think about your body energy account. Is it a healthy green or is it flashing red? If it's flashing red, you might want to revisit the energy bucket (see page 24) to identify what, if anything, may be acting as a drag on your energy resources as you reflect on the questions here:

- How healthy is your body energy account? Is it flashing green, red, or somewhere in the middle?

- If it's red, what are the consequences showing up in your life, eg chronic illness, fatigue, irritability, a hot temper?

- What can you do to bring your body energy account back into green and in credit?

- What will you focus on first?

- How does this translate into specific daily actions?

Brain/Body Synergy

The concept of synergy between the brain and body has evolved over time. Recent research has shone a light on the interconnectedness of brain and body and how changes in the brain affects bodily functions and vice versa. They work so seamlessly together that it's hard to separate them out, and over the past two decades, this has informed a much more holistic approach to health and wellbeing.

In fact, together, the brain and the spinal cord form the central nervous system (CNS): the spinal cord acts as an information superhighway, transmitting signals between the brain and body.

The Nervous System

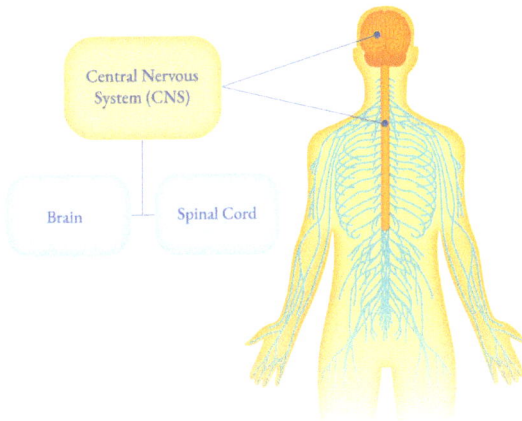

It plays a role in nearly every aspect of our health and wellbeing, with voluntary and involuntary bodily functions facilitated through a complex web of nerves known as the Peripheral Nervous System (PNS), which itself comprises two sub-divisions, namely the Somatic Nervous System and the Autonomic Nervous System.

The Nervous System

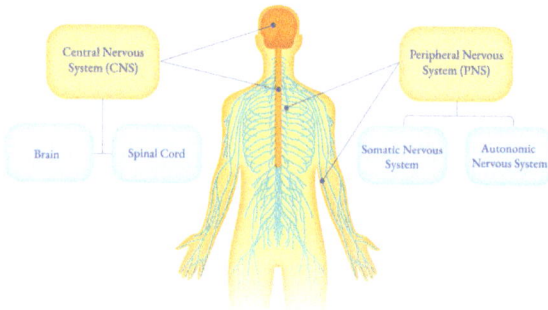

Somatic: Involved in the relay of sensory and motor information to and from the CNS. The activity is considered to be conscious or voluntary in nature.

Autonomic: Controls our internal organs and glands. The activity is considered to be outside voluntary control. The Autonomic Nervous System again splits into two parts, known as the Parasympathetic and Sympathetic systems.

The Nervous System

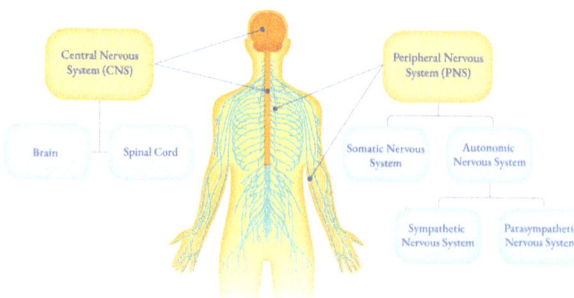

The Sympathetic system prepares the body to respond to what is recognised as 'stress-related' activity (eg increasing heart rate, slowing digestion and increasing sweat production).

The Sympathetic Nervous System

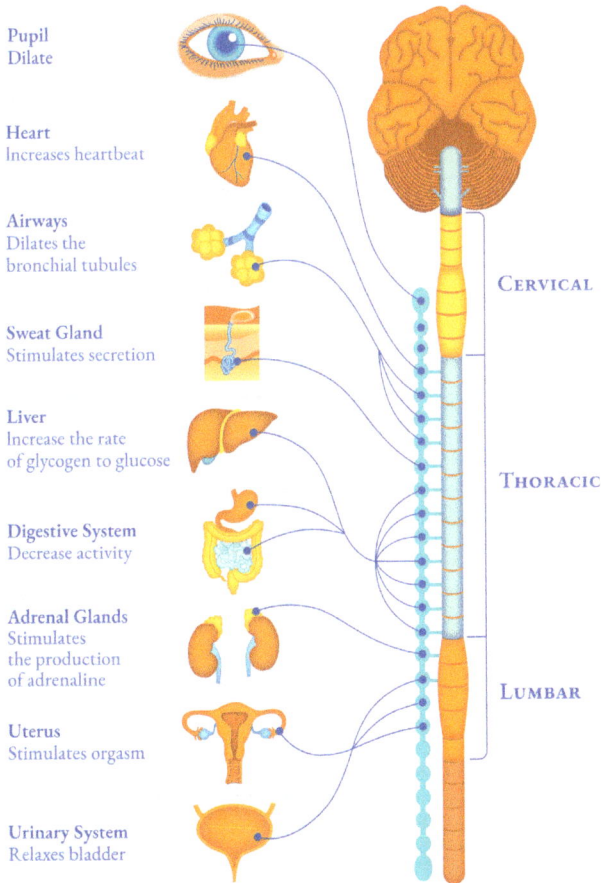

Pupil
Dilate

Heart
Increases heartbeat

Airways
Dilates the
bronchial tubules

Sweat Gland
Stimulates secretion

Liver
Increase the rate
of glycogen to glucose

Digestive System
Decrease activity

Adrenal Glands
Stimulates
the production
of adrenaline

Uterus
Stimulates orgasm

Urinary System
Relaxes bladder

CERVICAL

THORACIC

LUMBAR

Whereas the Parasympathetic system functions to return the body to a calm, relaxed state once the stress-related activity has passed by (eg heart rate and blood pressure decreasing, digestion increasing, pupils constricting).

The Parasympathetic Nervous System

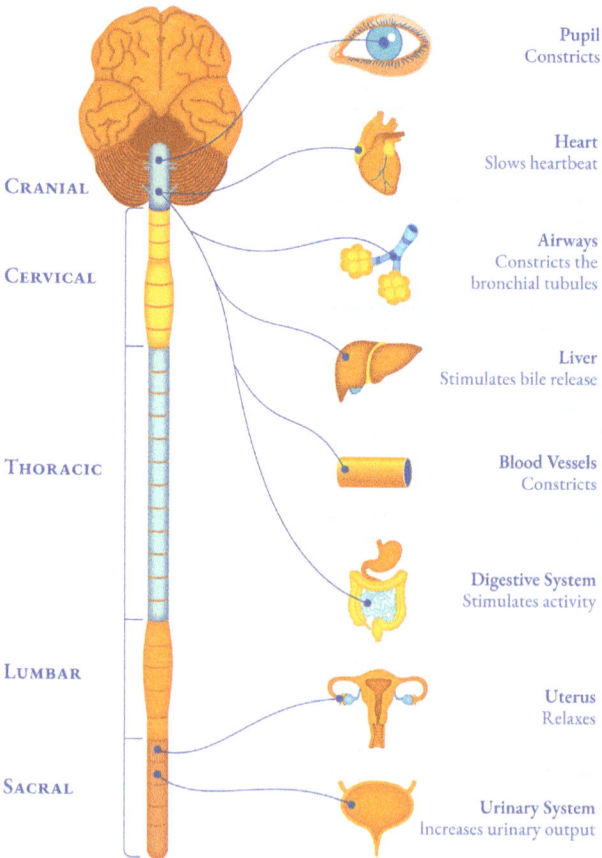

CRANIAL

CERVICAL

THORACIC

LUMBAR

SACRAL

Pupil
Constricts

Heart
Slows heartbeat

Airways
Constricts the
bronchial tubules

Liver
Stimulates bile release

Blood Vessels
Constricts

Digestive System
Stimulates activity

Uterus
Relaxes

Urinary System
Increases urinary output

These PNS nerves branch out from the spinal cord to every organ and body part, a seamless process that enables everyday activity, such as movement, as well as the regulation of autonomic processes such as heart rate, digestion, and breathing.

The PNS is integral to overall wellbeing, enabling the body to interact with the environment while maintaining all essential physiological functions. It is in our own interest to continually support a high functioning nervous system via good nutrition, exercise, hydration, and effective stress management.

This complex internal network of neural circuits that form the nervous system are continually evaluating risk – assessing every situation or person we encounter – to determine if we are safe, in danger, or in a life-threatening situation.

The detection of a person, an environment, or even the internal state of our body as unsafe, triggers a cascade of internal activity via the Sympathetic Nervous System. This often happens below our level of consciousness, thus preparing us for fight or flight by releasing hormones to boost the body's alertness and heart rate or by sending extra blood to the muscles ready for action. When the danger – real or perceived – has passed, the Parasympathetic Nervous System brings the body back to a calm state, slowing the heart rate, relaxing the muscles, and increasing intestinal and gland activity for rest and digest.

This process is known as neuroception and was first coined by Stephen Porges (Porges, 2004)[2], a professor of psychiatry and the director of the Brain-Body Centre at the University of Illinois.

Neuroception

Professor Porges states that even though we may not be consciously aware of danger, on a neurophysiological level, our body automatically begins a sequence of neural processes that can lead to fight, flight, or freeze. Depending on the sense of safety we feel from the world around us, many things will change within our nervous system. Our body literally transforms itself as different systems are activated. The state we are in becomes the lens through which we view the world.

Everything in our body is different, determined by how safe we feel, and feeling safe is crucial to our general health. When we feel safe, our heart rate slows, and we can hear and process tone of voice more effectively. Our facial muscles activate so that we appear more smiley and relaxed. We release beneficial hormones such as oxytocin, which enhances bonding and trust with others. We learn better, build better relationships, and are much more optimistic in our everyday life.

When we feel unsafe, our heart rate speeds up, and our pain tolerance increases. Muscles tense up, pupils dilate and we become hypervigilant as adrenaline and cortisol are released into the bloodstream. What this means on a day-to-day basis is that when we are anxious, running modern day challenges and issues through our old evolutionary systems, our nervous system can overestimate danger. This can create a downward spiral: if we don't take the time to think about and proactively manage this spiral, it can be difficult to escape it.

In life-threatening situations, even more things happen. We totally shut down. It's an instinctive, primitive response, and it explains why, when we're in extreme danger or suffering in conditions that are highly traumatic, we don't scream, we don't move – we remain motionless. It's involuntary, and it's our nervous system making the decision. Our conscious self has no say in the matter. Logically, we believe that if we were to find ourselves in an intensely frightening situation, we would run, move, shout, or scream. In reality, we don't. The nervous system takes over. We don't move. We don't make a sound: we literally remain motionless and soundless waiting for the danger to pass.

Until recently, it was believed that the body only had two responses: the ability to dial up in response to threat and then to dial down to calm our system, rest and digest. As a consequence of the work undertaken by Porges and his Polyvagal Theory (Porges, 2007)[3], this understanding has now shifted with the realisation that there is an additional response, recognised as a social engagement system. Central to this is something known as the vagus nerve, which plays an important role in regulating the social engagement system.

The Vagus Nerve

Similar to a thick electrical cord with many fibres, the vagus nerve originates in the brain and ends in the peripheral organs of the body. It has two main branches, one that sits to the front of the brain stem, called the ventral vagus, and one that sits to the back, known as the dorsal vagus. The ventral vagus is located above the diaphragm, with branches to the face, head, lungs, and heart, and it is referred to by Porges as our social engagement system.

Crucially, this system is not activated by thought – it is automatic and instinctive, operating from nerve influence and helps us navigate relationships, impacting who and how we interact. When we feel safe, the ventral vagus nerve runs the show, enabling us to engage and interact with others precisely because we feel safe enough to do so.

When we don't feel safe, the social engagement system shuts down via the ventral vagus nerve, and our older fight, flight, or freeze defence systems take over. This is important to note because to cultivate strong relationships and social connection, we have a deeply embedded biological requirement to feel safe. We are a social species and connectedness is integral to who we are, binding us together.

Feeling safe in our world, whether it be our home world, our work world, or our friendship world, is essential to us as human beings. We're not healthy or happy and we cannot maintain our cognitive performance when our unconscious neural processes light up electrical circuits to indicate safety has been breached. In such situations, the brain and body work together, transforming who we are, changing how we behave, what we feel, the sounds we hear, and even the tone of our voice.

Take a moment to consider how safe you feel within your different environments.

- Are you comfortable at work or suffering under a bullying boss?

- Do you have toxic friends who seem to always leave you feeling 'less than' instead of elevated and happy?

- Is there anything in your life that is currently impacting your sense of safety such as financial or relationship worries?

Take some time to reflect on your current situation. Is safety being breached? If so, how is it showing up in your behaviour, feelings, or responses? Understand that when we feel fearful or unsafe, it has a direct consequence on how we show up. The best way to regain balance is to move ourselves into a safer space. This might mean not seeing so much of a family member, letting a friendship go, or moving roles and/or company.

Consider what you might do to move yourself back to a safer situation. This may consist of small steps to begin with and that is OK. The most important step is awareness, understanding what might be contributing to our state and why, and then slowly working through what we can do about it.

Influencing the Nervous System

As we've discovered, understanding the nervous system and the brain/body connection increases our awareness of what happens largely below consciousness. The fact that everything happens mainly below consciousness, though, makes it difficult to actively influence the nervous system in the moment. Certainly, as we have learned, good nutrition, exercise, and sleep, among other factors all play an important role, as does working to protect ourselves as much as possible from toxic environments, people, thoughts, or situations, all of which negatively impact our sense of safety.

Be that as it may, what can we consciously do – to deactivate and calm the system in real-time – when the nervous system activates in response to an external or internal stressor? There are very few ways we can consciously influence the nervous system in the moment. However, there is one mechanism that is extremely powerful and works instantly, just like a light switch: the use of breath.

The Power of Breath

Breathing is the one of the automatic processes we can consciously control. The more we learn about it, the more we can consciously calm the nervous system when needed (Brown and Gerbarg, 2005)[4]. As we consciously alter breathing patterns, we directly influence both the physiological and psychological state because we're affecting the balance between the activation and deactivation branches of the nervous system.

Slow, deep breathing promotes relaxation, activating sensors in the lungs which slow the heart, reducing blood pressure and decreasing muscle tension to calm and deactivate the entire system. The longer the exhale, the more the sensors activate, directly sending messages to the brain, via the vagus nerve, that we are safe and all is OK.

Conversely, if we are in a situation where we need to energise our system, maybe before an important presentation or competition, we can consciously activate the nervous system using our breath. To do this, the inhale is longer and it is followed by a short exhale. Try both versions now and notice how your state alters, dependent on the length of the inhale/exhale combination:

- Short inhale/long exhale – deactivating (calm)

- Long inhale/short exhale – activating (ready for action)

Breathing techniques can be practised anywhere and are also commonly incorporated into yoga, meditation, and mindfulness practices. In my own experience, I have found the technique known as the physiological sigh (ScienceDaily, n.d.)[5] to be particularly effective.

The physiological sigh comprises two short inhales followed by a longer exhale. We tend to use this type of sigh in an involuntary way in everyday life, for example, when we are trying to calm our system following an outburst of tears. It's particularly noticeable when a child is experiencing the dying embers of a tearful episode. It can be used to our advantage in real time, it is very simple to do, and the more times we repeat the process, the calmer we feel.

Practising the Physiological Sigh

1. **Take two inhales in quick succession:** this reinflates the little sacs within the lungs that tend to deflate when we are stressed and carbon dioxide has built up in the blood stream.

2. **Follow the double inhale with a much longer and slower exhale:** this moves the diaphragm up; it makes the heart smaller and enables the blood to move more quickly, creating signals between brain and body that slows the heart down.

3. **Ideally breathe in through the nose and out through the mouth:** however, if this is not comfortable, do whatever feels right for you.

4. **Repeat as necessary:** do this until your system starts to calm down, returning to a more balanced state.

Deliberate breathing patterns are highly effective for balancing the nervous system and managing stress responses. Listening to mid-frequency music or soundscapes can also have a positive impact, albeit less potent than intentional breathing techniques. This auditory stimulation, including humming, activates the middle ear with the vibrations subtly benefitting the body (Golden et al., 2021)[6].

This might be because mid-frequency sounds are often found in nature – the rustling of leaves or the lapping of the ocean – or it could be because it stimulates the release of neurochemicals associated with pleasure and relaxation, such as dopamine and serotonin. Unlike high- or low-pitched sounds, mid-frequency sound is more closely associated with safety for the nervous system. Therefore, it resonates with the bones and tissues of the body and contributes to a sense of relaxation. Smiling and connecting with good friends, family, or work colleagues also has a similar effect.

Releasing Tension

Tension in the body often collects in the different muscle groups, contributing to an agitated, anxious state. Learning how to release the stored tension is a relatively easy skill to develop, and it enables us to benefit from a calmer physical system. In addition, as we release tension from the body, we also benefit from a calmer mind. When the body is tense, it's like having many tight knots in our muscles. These knots can send signals to the brain that something might be wrong or that we need to be on alert.

As a result, the mind can feel restless and anxious because it's getting the message that there might be a problem. However, when our body is relaxed, the brain gets the signal that everything is OK, and then it's much easier for the mind to calm and quieten our thoughts. A calm mind is necessary if we want to successfully engage in practices such as mindfulness. If the body is tense before we begin such practices, we will find calming the mind very difficult to achieve (Jacobson, 1974)[7].

Tension Release

Tension release is achieved by tensing certain muscles when breathing in and then relaxing them when breathing out. You might like to follow the process for relieving different muscle groups, developed by Shilagh Mirgain PhD and Janice Singles PsyD, 2016 (www.va.gov, n.d.)[8].

First, position yourself somewhere where you won't be interrupted, preferably where you can lie down, relax, and stretch comfortably. Then, work through the process outlined for each muscle group as shown in the following table.

- Breathe in and tense each muscle group holding for 4 to 10 seconds, avoiding pain and/or cramping.
- On the out breath, completely relax the muscle group.
- Wait 10 to 20 seconds and then move to the next muscle group.
- Notice how the muscles feel when tensed and when relaxed, including any differences.

The Muscle Groups	
Fists:	Clench both fists.
Biceps:	Bend elbows, tense bicep muscles.
Triceps:	Straighten arms, tense muscles in back of arms.
Forehead:	Wrinkle in a deep frown.
Eyes:	Close eyes tightly.
Jaw:	Gently clench jaw.
Tongue:	Press against roof of mouth.
Lips:	Press together and hold.
Neck:	Gently press neck back. Then bring head forward to chest and hold.
Shoulders:	Shrug shoulders as high as you can and hold stomach out as much as possible.
Lower Back:	Gently arch your back up.
Buttocks:	Tighten muscles in buttocks.
Thighs:	Tense by lifting legs off floor.
Calves:	Press toes downward, as if burying them in sand.
Shins and Ankles:	Bend feet towards head.

- If there is a particularly tense muscle group, repeat the exercise more than once.

The tension release activity is a great way to release tension from the body, and with practice, it can be completed within five minutes. However, if you find it does not work for you, there are other ways to release body tension. You might like to consider deep breathing techniques, stretching, activities such as yoga or Pilates, or taking yourself for a weekly massage. The important point to remember is that tension stores in the body; it lurks within the different muscle groups, causing physical discomfort and also heightening mental anxiety. The more we can release it, the better we will feel.

In Summary

- The body functions as the container through which we experience the world and the world experiences us.
- The brain and the spinal cord together form the central nervous system, with the spinal cord connecting and carrying information to and from the brain and all parts of the body.
- The nervous system plays a central role in regulating and coordinating virtually all of our bodily functions. It acts as the internal communication system, enabling different parts of the body to work harmoniously together.
- The nervous system is designed to activate when we are faced with threat and to deactivate to conserve energy and calm our system when the threat has passed.

- The ventral vagus (the branch that runs to the front of the brainstem and is located above the diaphragm with branches to the face, head, lungs, and heart) is an important third component of the autonomic nervous system.

- This third component is referred to as our social engagement system and this system is not thought-activated. It operates from nerve influence and helps us navigate relationships, impacting who we interact with and how.

- When we don't feel safe, the social engagement system via the ventral vagus shuts down and our older fight, flight, or freeze defence systems take over.

- Techniques such as breathing and managing the body budget better offer the opportunity to exert some conscious influence on the nervous system.

"Stress is like spice: In the right proportion, it enhances the flavour of a dish. Too little produces a bland, dull meal; too much may choke you."

Dr Donald Tubesing

Part Five

Stress Management

Introduction

Stress often gets positioned in the popular press and media as being inherently bad, something that inflicts untold harm on the human system. However, stress is a normal psychological and physiological reaction to the daily demands of life. When the stress response is functioning well, it provides the energy required for us to move into action, whatever that action may be.

Our nervous system is designed to activate the stress response to avoid danger, to perform, or to do something unexpected in the moment. It is then programmed to return to normal for rest and recovery. In other words, our nervous system guides us through an ongoing rhythm of activation peaks and deactivation troughs that enables us to confidently navigate the day. In this way, we have continual access to essential resources, with enough recovery time built in to ensure they are always available when needed.

It's worth remembering that without a well-functioning stress response, it would be virtually impossible to get out of bed in the morning. We need stress to function. That said, there are many situations within our social world that can trigger overactivation. In some ways, we are like the rest of the animal kingdom because our stress response activates when we are in physical danger. Unlike the animal kingdom, though, we humans can also think and perceive ourselves as stressed, even when in a perfectly safe space.

We can be safely sat at home, perhaps ruminating on mishaps at work or a particularly difficult conversation with a friend, and our stress response will activate. We can also observe unpleasant behaviour towards other people and, even if the behaviour is not directed at us, our stress response will also activate.

This ongoing activation often results in our system functioning with the stress button permanently flashing red, leaving us unable to deactivate sufficiently for rest and recovery. In our modern world, there are many contributing factors to our stress response. These can range from ongoing pressure at work or home and lack of sleep, to traumatic events and substance abuse. It is this switch from normal day-to-day stress activation to the permanently stuck-on-red chronic stress that causes the most harm to the human system. Unfortunately, if we are inattentive to what is happening within our system, we can easily slide towards a chronic stress state.

Our system is designed to keep us safe and well. Therefore, the brain is continually scanning the internal and external environment for potential threats whether they are physical, observed, or generated by our thoughts. Once a threat has been logged, the brain triggers a cascade of internal activity, which changes our internal physiology. This releases a cocktail of hormones and neurotransmitters into the body, activating the stress response and turbocharging the human system to mobilise the body for survival, manifesting through increased heart rate and blood pressure, slowing the digestive and immune systems, and tensing the muscles ready for action.

With chronic stress, these hormones and neurotransmitters continuously pump into the body, and it is this ongoing activation that causes the damage over time. Therefore, it's worth taking a moment to familiarise ourselves with the main hormones and neurotransmitters involved, what supports their activation, and what the potential consequences of overactivation are.

Hormones and Neurotransmitters

Hormone: a chemical messenger produced by certain parts of the body (for example, glands) that then travels through the bloodstream to regulate and control various functions in other parts of the body.

Neurotransmitter: a chemical substance that nerve cells use to send signals to other cells in the brain and body.

Cortisol (hormone): Cortisol is well-known for the role it plays in the activation of the stress response. However, it is also involved in mood and motivation as well as supporting the regulation of blood pressure and inflammation in the body. When we are experiencing the fight or flight response, cortisol has the capacity to shut down functions such as the digestive, immune, and reproduction systems, returning to normal functionality when the real or perceived threat has passed. When suffering with chronic stress, cortisol levels do not reset and this can lead to problems such as weight gain, headaches, heart disease, and depression.

Common causes of activation:

- Sense of threat; nervousness; anxiety
- Highly political environments; unhealthy competition
- Uncertainty; lack of autonomy; overwhelm
- Isolation; lack of belonging

Common consequences of overactivation:

- Impacts learning and executive thinking function
- Impairs ability to encode memory
- Disrupts ability to effectively regulate emotions
- Inhibits release of oxytocin – necessary for bonding, trust, and connection

Adrenaline (hormone/neurotransmitter): The body can react rapidly when adrenaline is released, with the changes experienced often referred to as an adrenaline rush. This boost of energy works to increase the heart rate, heighten the senses, and increase the breathing rate so that we are ready to leap into action to avoid danger. However, if adrenaline is released continuously, we end up feeling restless and irritable; the mind fills with anxiety and worry and we can suffer from broken sleep patterns and high blood pressure as a result.

Common causes of activation:

- Aerobic exercise
- Stressful situations

- Caffeine
- Fearful activity, eg riding a roller coaster

Common consequences of overactivation:

- Increased heart rate and blood pressure
- Anxiety and panic attacks
- Elevated blood sugar levels
- Chronic fatigue and a weakened immune system

Oxytocin (hormone): Oxytocin is often referred to as the bonding or love hormone and was originally considered a female only hormone. We now know that this is not true; however, oxytocin does play a very important role in social bonding as well as the modulation of fear and anxiety. When our bodies have high oxytocin levels, we experience feelings of trust, empathy, and connection because it reduces cortisol levels and promotes feelings of relaxation. When we become chronically stressed, oxytocin levels can become disrupted, leading us to feel more detached, leading to less social interaction and heightened anxiety.

Common causes of activation:

- Recognition for a job well done or a good performance
- Achieving challenging goals as a group
- Openness with peers, family, friends
- An enhanced sense of autonomy

Common consequences of disruption:

- Increased lack of trust

- Unwillingness to collaborate with others
- Reduced empathy impacting relationships and social bonding

Serotonin (neurotransmitter): Balanced serotonin levels are associated with feelings of wellbeing and play an important role in regulating not only mood but also sleep, appetite, and digestion. When chronically stressed, the brain finds it difficult to efficiently produce and deploy serotonin. This then negatively impacts sleep, appetite, and general overall health.

Common causes of activation:

- Social connection
- A sense of belonging
- Exposure to daylight
- A healthy diet and exercise

Common consequences of disruption:

- Increased levels of anxiety and/or stress
- Lack of motivation and increased apathy
- Low energy with an increasing sense of fatigue
- Disconnected relationships

Endorphins (neurotransmitter): Endorphins are the body's natural painkillers, often associated with the runner's high: the feeling of euphoria experienced after intense physical activity. In addition to supporting pain relief naturally, endorphins also act as mood enhancers. Chronic stress reduces endorphin production, which then results in an increase in our sensitivity to pain and heightened levels of emotional distress.

Common causes of activation:

- Bonding with those around us on a social level
- Laughter and a feeling of belonging
- Freedom to share emotion
- Moving the body

Common consequences of disruption:

- Increased level of anxiety
- Intensified low mood, leading towards depression
- Increased mood swings and impulsivity
- Difficulty sleeping

Dopamine (neurotransmitter): Dopamine is known as the 'feel good' or 'reward' chemical, and it plays a vital role in motivation, pleasure, and reward processing. It is crucial for attention, mood regulation, and coordinating smooth movements. With chronic stress, the dopamine pathways become disrupted, and this leads to reduced motivation. It can also leave you feeling tired and moody.

Common causes of activation:

- Thinking positively about the future
- Moments of insight and collaboration with others
- Clear, achievable goals
- Feeling that one matters and fair recognition for effort made

Common consequences of disruption:

- Increased tendency to procrastinate
- Lack of motivation
- Low energy
- Inability to focus attention

Understanding the Threat Response

Every stimulus the brain encounters is tagged as either safe (reward) or not safe (threat). That means that we either engage and approach or disengage and avoid, depending on how the brain chooses to tag the initial stimulus. This is exacerbated by the fact that we have evolved to be highly sensitive: we have become primed to notice threat over reward. This attraction or bias towards the 'bad' is thanks to our evolutionary journey. If we had not noticed threat when living in caves, we would not have survived as a species because there were just too many dangers.

Across thousands of generations, those who noticed threats lived to pass on their gene pool, whereas those who led lives where they were unaware of potential threats did not. Consequently, today we are highly sensitive to threat, which is why we notice five – some say nine – times more threats to rewards during our day-to-day activity. If left unchecked, that which evolved to keep us safe now has the potential to cause us considerable harm.

While there may not be as many life-threatening situations today, there are plenty of opportunities to identify threat within our social, family, and work lives, with enormous potential for triggering the stress response: speaking in public, frustration with goals, receiving feedback, redundancy, or falling out with a loved one. In such cases, stress activation is needed because it gives us the energy and motivation to navigate ourselves out of the perceived danger or difficulty.

However, once the danger or difficulty has passed, the stress response should deactivate. It is unfortunate, then, that in our modern world, we are prone to overthinking, rumination, and moving from one situation where we perceive threat to another. These perpetual cycles often do not allow for deactivation and a return to the normal base level.

It is this prolonged ongoing activation of the stress response that creates allostatic load (McEwen and Stellar, 1993)[1], meaning wear and tear on the body. This wear and tear – or allostatic load – increases the more the stress response is activated. As we now know, the continuous release of hormones and neurotransmitters dramatically impacts the body. However, the Yellow brain is also susceptible even to low levels of continuous stress activation.

In order to divert internal resources to the heart, muscles, and other organs ready for action, the brain must reduce the blood flow and oxygen it sends to the slower, logical Yellow brain. After all, we don't need to stand and think about what we are going to do: we just need to move. The consequence of this is that our ability to consciously think things out, pay attention, access memory, or exert cognitive control, is severely compromised.

While the process of activation is similar individual to individual, we don't all experience stress in the same way.

Stress thresholds vary from person to person, and it's in our interests to understand our thresholds and learn how to manage stress in a way that works for us and our life. In addition, with a certain amount of attention and practice, there is the opportunity to raise the stress threshold over time, increasing the comfort level when experiencing higher states of activation (see page 135 for more information).

How we think about stress and whether we believe we have the resources to deal with it plays an important role in this. If we believe that all stress is bad and we hold a 'stress is debilitating' mindset, then activation of the stress response will have a much greater impact on health, wellbeing, performance, and productivity than if we hold a 'stress is enhancing' mindset.

Stress as a Mindset

When we carry a belief that all stress is bad, the impact on the human system is more negative than when we accept stress activation as a normal and natural component of how we live and work (Peachy Essay, 2021)[2]. Take a moment to reflect and perhaps make a few notes in your notebook while considering the following questions:

- How do you view stress?
- Do you consider it friend, foe, or a mix of the two?
- How might your view on stress impact the way you feel and think?
- Does this influence your responses when you're in certain situations?

With greater awareness of our stress mindset, we have the option to choose the way we think about it. As we gravitate towards a more balanced mindset, the way stress expresses itself in the body will change – remember how closely connected the brain and the mind are.

Ongoing chronic stress certainly causes damage. However, as we get better at noticing the triggers and applying stress management techniques, we can radically reduce the causes of chronic stress alongside mitigating its impact. This is important because there is a direct link between heightened stress and performance. Ongoing chronic stress leads to a rapid deterioration of cognitive capability; however, normal stress activation heightens performance and increases motivation in the moment.

I have found it helpful over the years to remind myself that when I am behaving out of sorts, maybe displaying excessive emotion or unhelpful behaviours such as withdrawal, procrastination, or resistance to change, it's a sure sign that I'm heading towards or have reached chronic stress levels. The key is to notice the red flags and have a practised process to call upon for deactivating the rising anxiety.

Notice the Red Flags

Depleted resilience, overwhelm, and rising anxiety can show itself in many ways: extreme tiredness; repeated colds and ulcers; unexpected emotional outbursts; not to mention a whole plethora of addictions. Addictions themselves come in different forms, from the well-known reliance on alcohol or tobacco to the lesser-known need to binge on Netflix or shop-till-we-drop retail therapy jaunts.

Neither should we forget the increasingly common addiction to 'busyness', where we have become so accustomed to never switching off that sitting down for even five minutes with nothing to do is so uncomfortable that we immediately find something to busy ourselves with. When I start to consider rest and recovery a 'nice to have', I find it helpful to recall this simple equation.

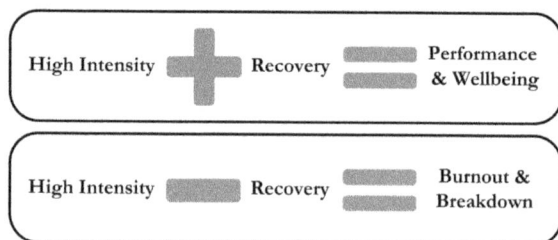

High Intensity ▨ **+** Recovery ▨ **=** Performance & Wellbeing

High Intensity ▨ **—** Recovery ▨ **=** Burnout & Breakdown

When we ignore the need for rest and recovery, the red flags appear in all manner of ways, indicating – sometimes screaming, even – that all is not well, that we need to slow the pace or make a change. These red flags could be annoying headaches that make us want to lie down, aches and pains in the neck and shoulders, irritability at the smallest of things, or a cacophony of thoughts that render sleep all but impossible.

Often the warning signs go unnoticed or worse – noticed and then consciously ignored. After all, there is so much to do. We can't stop now. That is until our system decides enough is enough and slams on the brakes, giving us the worst of migraines, a raging temperature, painful tonsilitis, or just collapses so badly that it is impossible to get out of bed and face the day.

I'm not sure what is worse, the predictable breakdown that directly impacts our health or the many relationships that have been destroyed along the way when we unnecessarily lost our temper or behaved unreasonably. Listening and responding to what the body is telling us is essential for rebalancing and regaining our equilibrium, for our own sake and also for all those around us.

Practise Raising the Stress Threshold

Proactively managing our stress threshold is simply the ability to consciously regulate what is going on in the brain and body: it is a process of learning how to calm the system when it has been activated. The higher the stress threshold, the more we can effectively manage how we respond to medium- or longer-term stressors such as work challenges, unexpected events, and illness.

To achieve this artificially, first, we must safely activate our system. We can achieve this in several ways: taking a cold shower, engaging in rigorous exercise, or participating in a minor anxiety-inducing activity to increase the heart rate. With an increased heart rate, we can then consciously practise slowing the heart down, using breath to bring ourselves back to a calmer state. The more we practise, the easier we can regulate ourselves in real time as we gently and safely develop a higher stress threshold.

You might find it helpful to follow the four-part structure, favoured by the Navy SEALs, illustrated here with the example of a cold shower:

Navy Seals Mental Training & Fear Framework	
1. Set your Goal:	How are you going to raise the heart rate? For example, by taking a cold shower (remember, never do anything to put yourself in danger or against your doctor's advice).
2. Mental Rehearsal	Ahead of your goal – getting under a cold shower – mentally visualise what will happen, including when you are going to take the shower; how you will feel as the body responds to the cold-water stressor; how you will bring your heart rate down through breath.
3. Self-Talk:	Notice your internal thoughts. What are you telling yourself before, during, and after? Is it all about can't or can, awful or learning? The internal narrative you generate will significantly impact your experience when in the shower.
4. Breathing:	When under the cold shower, consciously use your breath to slow the heart and calm the system. Breathe slowly with extended exhales. Breath is one of the most powerful and immediate tools we have for relieving the stress response in real time.

*Note: As with all **controlled** stress inducing activities, don't go for the full two or five minutes in the shower or throw yourself into a frightening challenge from the get-go! Start with a few seconds and work up to the goal you have set for yourself. Slow and steady is the name of the game. This is a marathon, not a sprint.*

Work the Waves

Part of the process of working to alleviate medium- to longer-term stress is to understand more about what's happening in the brain, so let's take a short journey through the wonders of the brain's waves. As we build our knowledge and understanding, it becomes clearer why certain activities such as mindfulness are so effective for managing stress or calming the human system more generally. I found that the more I understood the 'why' that sat behind such practices, the easier it became to cultivate and sustain those practices.

Very simply, our brains produce energy fields, known to most of us as waves. A brainwave is simply the pattern that neurons from across the brain make as they communicate with each other when they fire together. Modern day electroencephalograms (EEG) measure electrical activity in the brain using small metal discs or electrodes, which are attached to the scalp. These patterns are measured in cycles per second or Hertz (Hz), and there are five basic brainwaves.

Delta: Delta (0 to 4 Hz) is the slowest frequency, characteristic of deep, dreamless sleep.

Theta: Theta (4 to 8 Hz) is prevalent when in light sleep and/or dreaming. It's known as the frequency of rapid eye movement (REM) sleep.

Alpha: Alpha (8 to12 Hz) enables an ideal state of relaxed alertness and functions as the connector, connecting Gamma and Beta with Theta and Delta.

Beta: Beta, according to various researchers is in fact split into two waves: Low Beta (12 to 15 Hz), which is associated with a calm and peaceful mental state, such as daydreaming or reflective thinking; and High Beta (15 to 40 Hz), which supports problem-solving activity or any task that requires cognitive processing and concentration.

Gamma: Gamma is the highest brainwave frequency (40 to 100 Hz), and it is most active when we are learning, making

The Brain Waves

Frequency	Brain Waves	Brain State
Delta 0 – 4 Hz		Deep Sleep
Theta 4 – 8 Hz		Light Sleep
Alpha 8 – 12 Hz		Relaxed Alertness
Beta 12 – 40 Hz		Reflective/ Problem Solving
Gamma 40 – 100 Hz		Learning & Integrating

associations, or integrating information from across the brain.

It is fascinating that when we are fearful or highly stressed, the brain increases the levels of High Beta waves, impairing our ability to think rationally. As blood flow to the Yellow brain diminishes, the brain is then deprived of oxygen and essential nutrients and, consequently, our performance and health deteriorates. Dr Dawson Church describes this state of excessively High Beta activity as "the signature brain wave of a stressed-out consciousness".

It's also worth noting the importance of Alpha waves because they act as a bridge between the subconscious/unconscious Delta and Theta waves and the more conscious Beta and Gamma waves. The more Alpha we can generate or access, the more we connect our conscious thought with our intuition, embedded memories, and learning. This supports insight and the ability to connect fragile snippets of data together, moving brain performance into a higher zone of functioning.

But it all happens inside our skull, so what can we do about it?

As it happens – lots. We can alter brainwave patterns through certain practices. Meditation or mindfulness is known to increase Alpha and Theta waves; deep diaphragmatic breathing, tapping, or certain sounds such as binaural beats can also increase Alpha waves while reducing excessively High Beta. We can therefore consciously learn and practise how to shift our brainwaves. This is something top athletes and also people in the military learn to do, thereby supporting optimum performance.

Mindfulness: Research shows that practising mindfulness meditation can shift brain activity from high-frequency Beta waves to slower Alpha waves and even deeper Theta waves (Davidson et al., 2003)[3]. This shift in brainwaves promotes a sense of calm, enhances focus, reduces stress, and fosters overall wellbeing. You can find more information on mindfulness in the part on Mind.

Meditation: Regular meditation practice has been found to increase Alpha and Theta waves, which are associated with relaxation, focus, and creativity, while at the same time decreasing Beta waves that are linked to stress and anxiety. These changes in brain activity lead to improved cognitive function, increased self-awareness, and reduced emotional reactivity. Meditation also boosts the production of Gamma waves, which are associated with heightened alertness and enhanced overall brain function.

Note: While mindfulness and meditation are similar, there are some differences. We can be mindful without being in a state of meditation. Mindfulness is more about cultivating intentional awareness of the present moment and as such can be practised anywhere, whereas meditation is a more intentional, formal, time-structured practice, and it is often guided, in-person or online, to focus the attention.

Tapping: Tapping is also known as the Emotional Freedom Technique (EFT). By using the fingers to tap specific acupoints in sequence, we impact our brainwaves by stimulating specific acupressure points while focusing on an emotional issue or physical discomfort. Tapping supports brainwave transition from high-frequency Beta waves to the more relaxed Alpha and

Theta waves, thereby calming the brain's fear centre, leading to decreased stress levels and enhanced emotional wellbeing.

Binaural Beats: By listening to two slightly different frequencies in each ear, the brain perceives a third frequency known as the binaural beat. This can support the synchronisation of brainwaves. Listening to low-frequency binaural beats can stimulate Alpha and Theta waves, while higher frequency beats can enhance focus and concentration by stimulating Beta waves. However, it should be noted that reactions to beats can vary individual to individual. It's best to experiment to find one that best suits you, understanding that while some of us find the beats very effective, others can find them somewhat irritating.

Diaphragmatic Breathing: Deep breathing has a significant impact on brainwaves. When we engage in slow, deep breaths that expand the diaphragm, it signals the body to relax. This activates the Parasympathetic Nervous System, reducing stress and shifting brainwaves from high-frequency Beta waves to more relaxed Alpha and Theta waves. This shift promotes a sense of calmness, focus, and clarity, improving overall cognitive function and emotional wellbeing.

Neurofeedback/Biofeedback: Neurofeedback is carried out by trained specialists and involves the monitoring of brain activity through sensors which provide real-time feedback. It allows individuals to not only see their brainwave patterns but also to learn how to self-regulate and modify their brainwave patterns. Over time, the brain learns to produce more desirable brainwave patterns, leading to improved cognitive function, emotional regulation, and overall wellbeing. Neurofeedback has shown promising results in various conditions, including ADHD, anxiety, and depression.

Useful practices for reducing rising anxiety

Understanding more about the stress response, learning to develop our stress threshold, and managing our stress response in real-time is all good learning. However, to build resilience over the longer term, it's important to continue with all the things we know that are helpful such as good sleep, exercise, nutrition, gratitude training, and journalling. These practices and many like them enhance resilience and develop stress management capabilities.

The Navy SEALs mental training and fear framework is also helpful for quietening our fear response. Over time, if we engage in the four techniques (setting goals, mental rehearsal, self-talk, and breathe), we will notice that anxiety levels reduce and we generally feel calmer. In addition, there are other practices we can call on, some of which are detailed here for you to consider and perhaps apply day-to-day.

Labelling

The verbal labelling of negative emotion can help us recover emotional control. UCLA's Matthew Lieberman refers to this as "affect or mood labelling" and his fMRI brain scan research shows that this labelling of emotion appears to decrease activity in limbic structures such as the amygdala (Torre and Lieberman, 2018)[4]. This dampening of limbic structure activity allows the prefrontal (Yellow brain) thinking processes to exert greater influence, encouraging a considered response rather than an emotional reaction. Putting feelings into words has the same effect as pressing the brake on the car when we see a traffic light.

When we label our feelings using one word, we produce a rapid reduction in our automatic response to an emotional event by, for example, decreasing the heart rate and the amount of blood the heart pumps through the circulatory system. This internal unconscious activity puts distance between the rational, logical self and the emotion self, thereby calming us down.

There is also benefit over time. The research showed that participants with an extreme fear of spiders who engaged in labelling during an initial session with a live caged tarantula demonstrated greater decreases in skin conductance response during a second session one week later compared to patients who engaged in other emotion-regulation strategies such as distraction, reappraisal, or increased exposure.

Keep in mind that labelling is not the same as ruminating. We are labelling what we are feeling once using one word, two at most. We are not continually repeating that word to ourselves, which is unhelpful. Labelling is light touch; identify it, acknowledge it, and then let it go.

Third-Person Thinking

When we are anxious, distressed, or ruminating on painful experiences, talking to ourselves in the third person, (using non-first-person pronouns such as "you", "he", "she", or our own name), works to alleviate rising emotion without overloading cognitive resources. It is effective yet takes little effort (Moser et al., 2017)[5].

When we refer to ourselves in the third person, we think about ourselves as we would about others. This allows us to put distance between ourselves and the experience, helping us to better regulate the triggered emotion. Third-person self-talk improves emotional regulation without engaging cognitive control, which makes it a relatively easy regulation technique to call on.

Studies indicate that as we reflect or ruminate on painful emotional experiences and shift to think and talk in the third person, the activity in the brain regions associated with the pain felt quietens, thereby reducing the emotional activation. The third person can be used in many different situations such as:

- Preparing for a presentation: "You can do this; you know your stuff."

- Reflecting on an argument: "David, you overstepped the mark when you said what you said."

- Thinking about performance: "Joanna, if you had done your preparation, it would not have happened."

You might want to reflect on something that caused an emotional reaction and think it through in the third person. Notice how you feel and what additional observations, thoughts, or insights float to the surface.

The 'BEST' Framework

This framework (adapted from NeuroCapability)[6], can be used in the moment to remind ourselves of the key steps to deploy if we are starting to feel anxious or overwhelmed. A useful sentence to remember when anxiety starts to rise is, "Am I operating at my **BEST** right now?" This prompts the memory to recall the steps outlined here.

Be Aware: Notice what is happening. Is the jaw tensing, the heart racing, the palms sweating? Acknowledge that the emotion is rising and you are starting to feel anxious.

Emotional Control: Work to regulate the rising emotion. Use your breath to regulate the nervous system. Slow the breathing with a long, extended exhale.

Self-talk: Manage your thoughts. Be mindful about what you are saying to yourself and, if you begin to negatively ruminate, reframe and shift the thinking towards a more positive outlook using some techniques like the ABC method or practising gratitude.

The Two C's: The more we can **chunk** what is causing our anxiety down into bite-sized pieces or goals, the more structure we bring to the chaos. This enables our Yellow brain to work more effectively; it calms our system; it allows us to think out whatever is causing the anxiety. Finally, don't forget to **celebrate** the wins, no matter how small. Those shots of dopamine that facilitate celebration also support resilience and enables us to move forward to meet the next challenge with more confidence.

The BEST Framework			
Brain Aware	**Emotional Control**	**Self-Talk**	**The Two Cs**
• Notice what is Happening (within brain, mind, body)	• Work to Regulate (practise the learning)	• Manage Thought (negative to positive)	• Chunk & Celebrate (make it simple)
• Where/how is the impact showing?	• Slow breathing	• Halt negative thought patterns	• Reduce overwhelm
• Mood, body, pain, or tiredness?	• Labelling	• Shift mindset	• Chunk into small steps
• What might the brain be predicting?	• Third person thinking	• Get curious	• Celebrate along the way

The If/Then Framework

The If/Then framework (Gollwitzer and Sheeran, 2006)[7] enables us to think through and write out our responses to certain situations. By mapping this on paper ahead of time and focusing our attention when we are calm, in order to think or respond in a different way, we are more capable of halting automatic, heat-of-the-moment reactions.

The If/Then process gives us an opportunity to mentally rehearse how we will or would respond to situations and events: a mental preparation that helps us plan how to continue moving forward even when an obstacle presents itself. Whilst the If/Then framework can be used to support the achievement of many different goals, it is particularly helpful when we are learning how to adapt or respond to emotional or stressful situations.

As we grow and develop, we lay down many habitual ways of responding, embedding learned behaviours along the way. So when we find ourselves in times of high anxiety or chronic stress, we automatically revert to this learned behaviour, often resulting in inappropriate responses to the present-day situation. Various studies have demonstrated that creating If/Then implementation plans help us to not only respond quicker and more appropriately, but it also allows us to use fewer cognitive resources and less conscious thought in the moment.

Establishing the mental links we form through the process of If/Then planning means we can work towards our goals more automatically, helping us embed new habits with greater speed and efficiency. Professor Peter Gollwitzer labelled this process 'implementation intentions'. In a meta-analysis of the effectiveness of implementation intentions, Gollwitzer and Sheeran reported that findings from 94 independent tests showed that implementation intentions through the use of the If/Then framework delivered a positive effect of medium-to-large magnitude.

The If/Then process:

IF stands for the situational cue and **THEN** stands for the planned response to that cue: **IF** situation X arises, **THEN** I will do Y in response.

When we specify a situation (**IF**), we heighten an awareness of that situation. As a result, the situation and our responses become more noticeable to us and, as we recognise certain situations more easily, we can, in turn, attend to them better.

By mapping out our response (**THEN**), we form a link between a situation and how we will respond when faced with that situation. This enables us to act in the moment with less conscious effort. However, the value is in the detail. It is not enough to say, "**IF** X happens, **THEN** I am going to manage my emotions better." A plan of action must be created that includes the what, when, how, and why, mapped out such as, "**IF** X happens, **THEN** I will (what/behaviour) at (when/ time) in (where/location)." For example:

"**IF** I start feeling overwhelmed by my workload, **THEN** I will go for a walk outside every lunchtime to clear my mind and refocus. **IF** the situation continues after three days, **THEN** I will add 'workload' to the agenda for discussion with my manager during our Friday morning review meeting."

Log the Wins

Finally, we all have a natural tendency to gravitate towards what went wrong, while we discount, forget, or downplay what we did well. It's all thanks to that negativity bias that exists within all of us, which, unfortunately, contributes to a heightened fear response and increased stress activation. A way of mitigating the impact is to simply keep a note of our successes and wins as and when they arise. We can then refer to them, making it easy to recall all that we do well, reminding ourselves of what we have already achieved and how great we really are.

Use the following table and take a moment to consider something you have done well recently, something you are proud of. Use the table, or something similar, on an ongoing basis to keep a record of your achievements, and every time you find yourself doubting your capability or feeling your stress levels rising, take a moment to remind yourself of everything you have already achieved and that you are far more capable than you think.

The WINS Table

SITUATION	DESCRIPTION
Activity/Achievement.	
What did I do? How was I involved?	
What challenges did I face?	
What was the result of my effort?	
How did I feel?	
What did people say?	

In Summary

- Stress is a normal psychological and physiological reaction to the daily demands of life. When functioning in a healthy way, stress provides the energy required for us to move into action.

- Our nervous system is designed to activate the stress response when needed and then return to normal functioning, once the real or perceived danger has passed, for rest and recovery.

- In our modern world, we are prone to overthinking, rumination, and moving from one perceived threat situation to another, all of which have the potential to activate the stress response.

- Overactivation can lead to chronic stress, releasing a cocktail of hormones and neurotransmitters into the body, causing damage over time.

- Unfortunately, even though this response to stress evolved in order to keep us safe, it now has the potential to cause us considerable harm if left unchecked.

- A 'stress is debilitating' mindset has a greater impact on health, wellbeing, performance, and productivity than a 'stress is enhancing' mindset.

- We can choose the way we think about stress, managing its impact through learned techniques for regulating and calming the system when needed.

"If you want to go fast, go alone. If you want to go far, go together."

African Proverb

Part Six

Social Connection

Introduction

The final part on our journey is all about the importance of Social Connection, something that, when navigating our busy lives, we can unintentionally overlook – and yet it makes such a difference to our overall sense of happiness and wellbeing.

There is much research pointing to the enormous impact the effect of our social connections and relationships has on both our mental and physical health. Study after study demonstrates that fostering social ties can result in decreased rates of anxiety and depression, enhanced self-esteem, and even a potential 50% boost in life expectancy (Blum 2012)[1]. The research goes even further, indicating that a lack of meaningful connections can result in health implications considered to be more serious than smoking, high blood pressure, or obesity. This can ultimately lead to increased cellular inflammation and a heightened risk of various health issues.

We have evolved over millennia to respond to connection; it is the social nature of who we are, resulting in a brain finely tuned to emotional states. So much so that the brain has evolved with a network of interconnected neurons, all working together to facilitate learning, helping us understand the action and behaviours of those we observe. Research is ongoing; however, this mirror neuron system is considered fundamental to what it means to be human (Penagos-Corzo et al, 2022)[2].

Evidence suggests mirror neurons support observation, visualisation, and representation (Woolfolk, 2020)[3], and they are more likely to fire when we understand the other person's goals or intentions (Eysenck & Keane, 2015)[4]. This ability to facilitate imitation helps us learn social behaviours and build rapport through mimicry. In addition, when we witness someone else's joy or sadness, our mirror neurons are likely to fire, creating a shared emotional experience.

While we can't say that this system is associated with all action understanding, or empathy-related activity, mirror neurons are considered to play an important role in the process. They contribute to our understanding, empathy, and compassion, allowing us to connect on a deeper level.

Whether it's interpreting facial expressions, mirroring body language, or intuiting intentions, these neurons play an important role in our ability to connect emotionally, communicate effectively, and build meaningful relationships in the complex social fabric that is human society.

So much of what it means to be human is to be social. Charles Darwin himself noted the importance of compassion and kindness for survival in his theory of evolution. He is often remembered for the much-quoted "survival of the fittest".

However, this phrase did not originate with him. It was actually generated in 1864 by Herbert Spencer and his group of Social Darwinists who used Darwin to justify their desire to attribute superiority to certain classes and races.

Darwin was much more intrigued about the importance of tribe, of the need for belonging, and connection for survival. In fact, it is said that "survival of the kindest" better captures Darwin's thinking about the natural process of mankind. Darwin did use the phrase in the fifth edition of *On the Origin of Species* in 1869, though he is said to have viewed "survival of the fittest" merely as a synonym.

More recently, data from a Harvard study of 724 men, which began in 1938 and spanned an 80-year period, demonstrated the importance of relationships (Robert Waldinger, 2016)[5]. This was demonstrated particularly in the health of our general day-to-day relationships, which is a fundamental factor that keeps us happy as it is these relationships that protect us from upheaval and help us to stay resilient during change – more so than money, fame, social class, IQ, or even genes. At the end of the day, it does not matter who we are, where we work, or what we do, the more we invest in quality connection, inclusion, and relationship, the happier we feel and the higher we perform.

Notice Rising Exhaustion

The consequences of social isolation are significant, with loneliness, isolation, and alienation said to be on the rise. Indeed, these symptoms currently hold the dubious honour of being among the highest ranked reasons why so many individuals seek psychological counselling. Tiredness and exhaustion can be considered as early warning signals for the need to repair social connections and relationships.

When we are socially disconnected, we experience heightened levels of anxiety, and these negative emotions contribute to feelings of mental and physical exhaustion. Whereas when we are socially connected, we benefit from external support, companionship, and a sense of belonging, helping us navigate challenging situations and cope with stress.

Just as diabetes disrupts our ability to self-regulate the level of sugar in the internal environment of our blood, loneliness can disrupt our ability to self-regulate in the external social environment (Hackett, Hudson, and Chilcot, 2020)[6]. As our thinking and behaviour become more and more disrupted, the lonelier we are.

A study undertaken by the University of Vienna and published in *Psychological Science* (Stijovic et al., 2023)[7] found that people who experienced social isolation for eight hours reported higher levels of tiredness, suggesting that low energy may be a basic human response to a lack of social connection.

Don't Underestimate Social Pain

Often, social pain is not viewed as seriously as physical pain, yet it is experienced on similar brain networks. The main difference is that social pain can last much longer and run much deeper than physical pain. If you have ever broken a leg, arm, or similar, you will know that when recalling the event 10 years later, you can remember the discomfort but not the visceral pain of the actual break.

'Social pain can last much longer and run much deeper than physical pain.'

However, if we experience a fallout with a good friend that resulted in deep hurt, it can often move us to the same level of anger, upset, or shame 10 years later, just as it did on the day it happened. We relive the visceral nature of social pain in a way that we don't experience with physical pain. This is particularly so if we have not undertaken the internal work to heal the pain and forgive whatever happened to us.

It is strange then that our response to physical pain usually comprises lots of support, sympathy, and condolences. Yet when we or others experience social pain, we're usually offered a cup of tea or a bar of chocolate (if we are lucky) and told it will be OK in a day or two. The attention and concern of others wanes quickly though our social pain is often deeper and more long-lasting.

Maybe this is because we can't physically see what's broken, therefore we don't give it as much attention or care. Maybe the subject matter is so sticky or complex that we feel uncomfortable listening or being there for the other person. Maybe we are just unaware and underestimate the significance of social pain. There can be many reasons; however, it is worth remembering that social pain is very real. It has been proven that we can really die from a badly broken heart (Sethi et al., 2022)[8].

Social pain demands that we are kind to ourselves and/or others – that we don't ignore it or pretend it is not happening. We may need to sit with the pain for a while and find a way to understand it and accept it so that we can begin the journey of healing. As we heal and find a way to forgive, the pain loses its power. Whereas the more we hold on to it, turning it over in our mind – or the more we try to ignore it – the more powerful and disruptive it gets.

This resistance to working through social pain leaks out into our attitude and behaviours, impacting our future life and relationships. It's not healthy and it's counterintuitive: the more we can process and forgive whoever or whatever caused us social pain, the happier we are; the more we hold onto the anger and upset, the unhappier we are. Really, the only person we end up hurting is ourselves. That is no way for us to live.

Take a moment to consider:

- Is there any current or residual social pain in your life right now?
- How often are you turning this pain over in your mind?
- What do you feel in your body when you recall what happened?
- What do you need to help you reframe what happened and/or find a way to forgive? (This may involve talking to a friend; seeking professional help; writing a letter to the other person; journalling; working it through via mindfulness practice or meditation)

- If you behaved badly or spoke out of turn, then consider sincerely apologising – it may not save the relationship; however, it will clean the slate and allow you to move on.

Be kind to yourself. Remember that by holding onto social pain the only person you are hurting is you. Take your time with it. It is a process. It is not something that is usually fixed in five minutes. As you work through it, with the benefit of distance, perhaps using techniques such as third-person thinking (see page 143) or engaging the support of a coach or similar, you will release the blockage and set yourself free.

It took me many years to let go of the pain and the deep sense of abandonment that had sat with me since childhood. I was angry for a long time and lived in an unforgiving mood. It got in the way of my ability to love myself and form meaningful relationships with others. It was only when I forgave those involved and released the anger that I was able to heal and move forward.

Do I see those people now? No.

Have I forgiven all that happened? Yes.

Will we have a relationship going forward? No… and that is OK.

Some individuals are not meant to be in each other's lives, and this applies to blood relatives as much as it does friends and acquaintances. However, I carry no ill will, no regret, and no 'if only'. It is what it is, and after much reflection and the support of an excellent coach, I was able to accept that and move forward in peace, being grateful for what I had become.

During the process and into the present, I have found the following heart/mind harmony exercise (courtesy of The Institute of Heart/Math) helped me tremendously, particularly when I began to ruminate on the past, causing anxiety to rise. Slowing and focusing on the breath influences the Autonomic Nervous System (see page 114), synchronising and harmonising the heart's electrical activity with brainwaves. Visualising the breath carrying love into the heart and anxiety out of the heart, while not scientifically grounded in either anatomy or physiology, is a powerful addition, shifting the focus towards more healing and expansive feelings of joy and gratitude.

If you would like to try the heart/mind harmony exercise, first find somewhere where you can sit comfortably.

- Take a deep breath in, hold it at the top, and then release.

- Close your eyes and move your hand to your heart.

- Keep breathing, gently shifting your attention to the heart; imagining, or sensing, that you are breathing in and out through the heart.

- Imagine, or sense, your heart expanding with each in-breath and relaxing with each out-breath.

- As you breathe, imagine that on each in-breath you are drawing in joy, love, and compassion, and on each out-breath, you are releasing tension and/or anxiety from the body.

- Continue for roughly 60 to 90 seconds, then take a final deep breath, roll your shoulders back, and open your eyes.

How do you feel?

If the exercise is new to you, my recommendation is that you do it five times a day for seven days. This creates a link in your mind between your hand moving to the heart and the mind/body system shifting into harmony. Eventually, as the connection strengthens over time, all you will need to do is put your hand to your heart for that same shift to occur. As you become more used to the practice, you don't need to close your eyes and you'll be able to do it anywhere: on the train, waiting in line for a service, or just sitting in the park.

It's simple, yet effective.

Connecting with Others

We might think that if we are more introvert, there is not the same need to connect with others. Well, it is true that perhaps those of us who are introvert might not need as much social connection; we may just connect in different ways; however, regardless of whether we are introvert or extrovert, we all have an in-built need to connect in some way. Connection is so much more than a numbers game. We can have many friends and associates and yet still feel desperately disconnected and lonely in the middle of it all.

Feeling connected, then, is a subjective experience. It's more about how we feel inside – the health and happiness of our internal state. As Emma Seppälä stated in her 2013 TEDx, (www.youtube.com, n.d.)[9], we don't always have full control over our external environment; we can't always change how many friends we have, but we do have a say over our internal state and how connected we do or do not feel with the world around us. This is something we can work on regardless of whether we connect in different ways, in different numbers, or at different times of the year, month, day, or night.

Importantly, we don't need to change anything to connect with ourselves. We are beautiful, worthy, and good enough just as we are. It does not matter how we look, what we weigh, or how many qualifications we do or don't have. What matters is how much we love ourselves and the care and kindness we show to ourselves – in other words, how much self-compassion we have for who we are. This, as we discussed at the very start of this journey, matters more than anything else in the world. It matters more than money, more than fame, and more than spectacular life experiences. We can be surrounded by the best of everything, but if we don't love who we are, it's not worth anything.

Conversely, we can have practically nothing and love ourselves every day and everyday life will find simple ways to reward us. The problem in our modern age is that many of us judge our worth and value by what we own. It's a sad road to nowhere. We have lost the ability to just love who we are. Instead, we continually compare ourselves with others, usually via social media, and almost always find ourselves lacking. We don't earn enough. We are not beautiful enough. Our car is not big enough. Our home is not full of enough. And so on it goes.

Sometimes we think the ability to be compassionate for ourselves or others is beyond us. This is far from the truth. Research suggests compassion for self and others is innate (García-Campayo et al., 2023)[10]. The Max Planck Institute for Evolutionary Anthropology, Leipzig, Germany, undertook work with two-year-olds and observed they were eager to help others before they even understood what compassion was (Warneken and Tomasello, 2006)[11]. In addition, Professor Dale Miller at Stanford found that while our first instinct is to share, we sometimes stop ourselves in case people think we are self-interested (Miller, D. T.,1999)[12]. This is a mistake because the more compassion we show for ourselves, the more we show for others and the more resilient we are in the face of different challenges.

Self-compassion is a source of enormous strength and it's hugely contagious. Professor Nicholas Christakis at Harvard found that if one person acts fairly, it impacts others three degrees of separation away from them. In other words, the more compassionate we are in our own life, the more it helps our family, neighbours, and work colleagues to be compassionate in theirs. Compassion influences our internal state; it helps us feel more connected, reaping the benefits from that connection.

So how do we achieve it?

Give, share, offer support, and, crucially, learn to be kind and love ourselves just as we are. In Self-Care, you were introduced to a self-compassion exercise, and I would ask you to revisit this and perhaps pay even more attention to it. In fact, I would ask you to get into the habit of practising ways to love yourself every single day because the more you love yourself, the more you connect with the world around you. In addition, you can get involved in activities such as volunteering or practise different ways of expanding your compassion – for example, engaging in random acts of kindness.

Volunteering

Volunteering delivers huge health benefits: it reduces cortisol and alleviates stress while amplifying positive emotions. It can be a powerful means to create social connection as we have the opportunity to connect with people within the community who share common interests or aspirations. Working together for a common goal creates a sense of purpose and accountability, increasing social engagement and social capital (Nichol et al., 2023)[13].

A volunteer project also provides opportunities to meet people from diverse backgrounds, increasing social awareness and the understanding of different perspectives. The positive sentiment associated with helping others is hugely enhanced through volunteering. It is a win-win situation in promoting social cohesion by enhancing community wellbeing while benefiting the physical and mental state of the volunteers themselves.

Random acts of kindness

Kindness is something that materially costs nothing yet continually increases in value the more it is shared (Melamed D., et al, 2020)[14]. It is a transformative force with study after study showing that the kinder and more compassionate we are, the happier we are. Kindness promotes gratitude and empathy as well as a sense of interconnectedness with others, strengthening our sense of community and belonging.

When we perform kind acts, whether it's holding the door for someone, offering a helping hand, or simply expressing gratitude, we create a positive ripple effect which impacts ourselves and the person to whom we are showing kindness. We release the hormones and neurotransmitters dopamine, serotonin, oxytocin, and endorphins that contribute to our sense of happiness. The kinder we are to friends, acquaintances, or strangers, the more we benefit ourselves. It is indeed a truism that the more we smile at those around us, the more the world smiles back at us.

Happiness is a Social Thing

Ultimately, wellbeing and happiness is derived from relationships, connection, and great social experiences. The joy of a new car may last a day, a week, or a month; however, the joy from a great holiday with friends can last months, years, and sometimes decades.

How many times have you planned a trip away, laughed, and discussed what you were going to do ahead of departure date, had a wonderful time whilst away, and years later were still crying with laughter at the memories? Or how often do you sit around the dinner table with partners, friends, or family, laughing and talking about something that seemed like a crisis at the time, yet looking back with the passage of years, provides a whole night's entertainment?

There is more happiness in a night out with a good friend or friends than will ever be realised through the purchase of something. Does this mean we should not desire nice things? Not necessarily. We can all desire to be surrounded by lovely things and enjoy them when we have them. However, it's important to understand that whilst these purchases may be pleasant and comfortable, such things do not make us happy. They may contribute to an already happy life, but adding such things to an unhappy life will not turn that unhappy life into a happy one. That requires something very different.

It requires the small changes we make every day as we adjust our mindset, behaviour, and habits in ways that ripple out, impacting all we do and all we are. It's what this book is about: all the day-to-day things we can do to stay well and in balance, all the small shifts and changes that enable us to process the external world in a different way, thus enabling us to adjust our inner world and to find joy in the smallest of things in unison with a sense of peace and fulfilment.

As researcher Professor Dan Gilbert states, we have a strong tendency to overestimate the impact of life events, when in reality, extreme positive or extreme negative events don't influence long-term levels of happiness as much as we think they do (Gilbert, 2009)[15]. In a 1978 study published by researchers at Northwestern University, it was discovered that the happiness levels of paraplegic individuals and lottery winners were essentially the same within a year of their respective life event occurring (ResearchGate, n.d)[16].

Yet if we were asked to predict happiness levels, we would incorrectly predict that lottery winners are more likely to be happy whilst paraplegic individuals are more likely to be unhappy. More recent studies have come to similar conclusions showing that people who have undergone major life trauma experience little impact on happiness levels three months after the event took place. Exceptions are few and far between. How can this be true?

It happens because we tend to revert to our happiness baseline regardless of what is happening around us. A lottery winner may feel immediately happy when they think about what they are going to spend their money on; however in reality, 99% of their life – unless they make a conscious effort to change habits, mindset, and behaviour – will not have changed. Therefore, after the initial high, happiness levels will simply revert to their original baseline. Likewise, when something bad happens, once the initial shock has passed, happiness levels revert to that person's original baseline.

This is because we are more than a joyful or dreadful event that happened to us: we are the sum of many different things. It is this, not exceptional events – whether they be positive or negative – that determines happiness levels. The keys to shifting our happiness, therefore, are not external to us, they are within our control, in the form of our habits, mindset, and behaviours.

For this reason, we perhaps need to think about happiness and how we generate happiness in a different way. Professor Gilbert describes two roads to happiness: natural happiness, which spontaneously arises when we get what we want; and synthetic happiness, which we generate day after day regardless of whether we get what we want or not.

It is interesting that many of us continually search for a form of natural happiness, and yet we now know that the brain simply does not work that way. When we get what we want, the brain adapts and moves us on to wanting something else. This is known as hedonic adaptation and essentially makes the experience of happiness brief while long-lasting happiness always remains just out of reach. It reflects the brain's skill at adapting to what we have and the situations we find ourselves in.

Every time we achieve something such as passing an exam, buying the car we always wanted, or earning a pay rise, the brain adapts itself, turning what we achieved into the everyday and normal. This means the happiness we feel rapidly dissipates. In fact, we can create too much wanting, which then leads to a form of addictive unhappiness as we continually strive for the "new this" or the "upgraded that", misguiding us into thinking it will make us happy.

Synthetic happiness, on the other hand, is something we have to generate from nothing for ourselves, particularly when we don't get what we want. We have to remind ourselves of what we are grateful for, recall how we enjoy our friendships, savour past wins, and remember what is good in our life. It is not easy. It takes effort, and it's not something we can accommodate when stressed, exhausted, or generally out of balance within ourselves.

There is a natural tendency to think that natural happiness is superior to synthetic happiness. This is a false belief. Natural happiness relies more on what is happening external to ourselves, and this is something we often have little control over – meaning we are in danger of being buffeted about by life events. Whereas when we generate synthetic happiness internally for ourselves regardless of what is happening externally, it's a skill that we can cultivate, practise, and manufacture for our benefit over time. Best of all? It's open to all of us.

As a footnote, there is a belief that happiness is completely tied into the genes we were born with, therefore making it virtually impossible to change experienced happiness. Certainly, genes do play a part in determining baseline happiness levels. According to Sonja Lyubomirsky and her book, *The How of Happiness* (Lyubomirsky, 2007)[17], genes influence the happiness we experience by up to 50%, with external circumstances accounting for 10%. This still leaves 40% for us to work with. That is a big chunk that we can influence. Happiness rarely happens by accident. The more we connect, the more we care for ourselves, the more we work with the brain's ability to change, the more we can create more happiness in our lives.

Final Thoughts: Avoid Social Comparison

It is inevitable that we will compare ourselves to others, regardless of whether that is within our social environment, home, work, or our friendship groups. After all, it helps us set our social compass, to understand where we fit within our group. However, as the influence of TV, social media, and glossy magazines has increased, so has the danger that our social compass runs incorrectly, particularly if we don't manage our exposure to such external media.

Unfortunately, if we continue to compare ourselves against impossible external references, we will always find ourselves wanting. We can never match up and, consequently, regardless of who we are or how well we are doing, our happiness level will deteriorate rapidly. If we are continually exposed to photographs of beautifully sculpted models, then satisfaction with our normal human body can plummet, even though we know logically that the photographs are airbrushed and unrealistic. If we go on Facebook and see thousands of posed pictures of people on holiday in exotic places and then compare it to our quiet staycation with our family or friends, we may start to feel that our life is in some way inferior.

Too much social comparison with the unattainable is a killer for wellbeing. I'm not saying we should shut everything down and come off social media – that would be almost impossible in the online world we now occupy, and it would also mean missing out on a lot. That said, we can make a conscious effort to perhaps reduce the external stimuli we expose ourselves to, maybe apply some filters, and have more consideration regarding where we focus our attention. What is it they say? Everything in moderation.

In Summary

- A healthy brain, mind, body, and effective stress management sit within the wider context of social connection.

- The human system has evolved over millennia for connection, with social connection delivering many health benefits including lower rates of anxiety and depression.

- Lack of connection is considered worse for our health than smoking, high blood pressure, and obesity.

- Just as diabetes disrupts our ability to self-regulate the level of sugar in the internal environment of our blood, so loneliness can disrupt our ability to self-regulate in the external social environment.

- Social pain is often not viewed as seriously as physical pain, yet it is experienced on similar brain networks. The main difference is that social pain can last much longer and run much deeper than physical pain.

- Feeling connected is a subjective experience; it's more about the health and happiness of our internal state. This is something we can all work on regardless of how we choose to connect and regardless of whether we are introvert or extrovert.

- Self-compassion is a source of enormous strength and it's hugely contagious. The more compassion we show for ourselves and others, the more resilient we are in the face of different challenges.

- Happiness can be synthetic or natural, and the ability to generate synthetic happiness is a skill that can be developed by everyone.

- Social comparison is a happiness killer. The more we compare ourselves, the more likely it is that we will find ourselves wanting. Try and moderate your exposure to this kind of content.

Conclusion

So here we are. We've reached the conclusion of our journey together. I hope you are madly in love with yourself, understand more about yourself, and are enjoying the person you are becoming.

The book may be complete, but I'm sure you know that the journey does not end here. There is no such thing as leaving ourselves to our own devices. We must continuously care for ourselves, set those boundaries, steer ourselves away from negativity, and be clear on what is OK and what is not OK for us. Remember, the brain has no moral code. It will simply wire and rewire itself according to where our attention goes. It's our choice to be grateful for what we have or not; we can choose to celebrate the connections and relationships we make or not; and we can choose to love ourselves or not.

My hope for you is that you have really started to look after your beautiful self, that you have taken the tools and techniques you need to lead your best life. That is not to say life is easy or that challenges, disappointments, or grief never come. They do; however, I hope you realise that whatever comes your way, everything you need to work through it already exists within you.

Just remember that it is very difficult to access those resources when we are tired, hungry, overwhelmed, or suffering from chronic stress. It's nothing to do with being 'less than' and losing your temper with someone doesn't inherently make you a bad person; simply take it as a sign that your system is out of balance. It's exhausted, spent, out of juice – it needs some love, care, and attention. Then you'll find it will rebalance, and your wonderful self will once more shine through.

So please, do keep moving forward. Don't beat yourself up if you have a bad day, week, or month. It happens to all of us. Just stand back up, dust yourself down, and start all over again.

If you haven't done so already, you might want to redo the Stay Well Assessment in the Self-Care part. Notice how your scores have shifted, what is different, and what might have impacted those scores. Reflect on the work you have done and notice how you are feeling now. I regularly revisit the assessment as it keeps me focused on where I might need to pay particular attention, especially during busy periods.

As I said right at the beginning, I am continuing on my journey, and while I may still fall over, I fall over a lot less than I did, and I'm miles on from where I started. When you look back in six months or a year, you will be able to notice how far you have travelled.

Do let me know how your journey goes. I love hearing all the stories, and if you need some support, just drop me an email on deborah.hulme@minervaengagement.com. You know where I am.

Resources & References

Programmes to support your Thrive Well journey:

Now that you know it's possible to Thrive Well, and that you can stay healthy and happy regardless of changing circumstances, you may want to learn and understand even more. To speed your progress we've created the following programmes to provide support over and above the book alone.

Thrive Well Learning

During this on-line learning programme, you are personally guided in applying the principles, habits and tools outlined in the book, to immediately impact what you do and how you do it.

Thrive Well Coaching

The coaching programme is designed to assist you in integrating the Thrive Well habits into everyday life, helping you develop new strategies for thinking, feeling and acting in a way that supports you to stay well and perform well.

Thrive Well Speaking

Having delivered countless presentations and keynote addresses to businesses, professionals and nonprofit organisations, I know how such activity galvanises audiences into action. I'm always grateful for the opportunity to inspire and transform thinking around wellbeing and performance.

Thrive Well Community

Join our Thrive Well Community for the opportunity to meet like-minded individuals, share experiences and benefit from ongoing support and connection.

For more information on these and other activities, please visit:
www.minervaengagement.com/thrivewell

Books:

1. Authentic Happiness: Using the New Positive Psychology to Realise your Potential for Lasting Fulfillment, by Martin Seligman (Free Press, 2004).

2. Change your Brain, Change your Life: The Breakthrough Programme for Conquering Anxiety, Depression, Anger and Obsessiveness by Dr Daniel G. Amen (Piatkus, 2016).

3. Flow: The Psychology of Optimal Experience by M. Csikszentmihalyi (Harper and Row, 2008).

4. Mind to Matter: The Astonishing Science of How Your Brain Creates Material Reality by Dawson Church (Hay House UK, 2019).

5. The Body Keeps the Score: Brain, Mind, and Body in the Healing of Trauma by M.D. Bessel van der Kolk (Penguin Books, 2015).

6. The Happiness Advantage: The Seven Principles that Fuel Success and Performance at Work by Shawn Achor (Virgin Books, 2011).

7. Thinking, Fast and Slow by Daniel Kahneman (Farrar, Straus and Giroux, 2011).

8. You Are Not Your Brain: The 4-Step Solution for Changing Bad Habits, Ending Unhealthy Thinking, and Taking Control of Your Life by Jeffrey Schwartz and Rebecca Gladding (Avery, 2012)

Helpful Websites:

1. Emotional Freedom Technique (EFT): EFT uses gentle tapping on key meridian points on the body to release emotional, health or performance issues (www. tappingsolutionfoundation.org).

2. The Insitute of HeartMath: The mission of HeartMath is to establish heart-based living and global coherence by inspiring people to connect with the intelligence and guidence of their own hearts (www.heartmath.com).

3. The Work: A simple, powerful process of enquiry that teaches you to identify and question the stressful thoughts that cause suffering (www.thework.com).

4. Functional Shift: Providing healthcare for the whole person. A roots and branch approach that addresses Mind, Body and Meaning (www.functionalshift.com)

References

Chapter One: Self Care

1. National Human Genome Research Institute (2022). *Human Genome Project.* [online] Genome.gov. Available at: https://www.genome.gov/about-genomics/educational-resources/fact-sheets/human-genome-project.

Chapter Two: Brain

1. Ampel, B.C., Muraven, M. and McNay, E.C. (2018). Mental Work Requires Physical Energy: Self-Control Is Neither Exception nor Exceptional. *Frontiers in Psychology*, [online] 9.doi:https://doi.org/10.3389/fpsyg.2018.01005.

2. Anon, (n.d.). *The Neuroscience of Active Learning – Writing Across the Curriculum.* [online] Available at: https://openlab.citytech.cuny.edu/writingacrossthecurriculum/2015/10/15/the-neuroscience-of-active-learning/.

3. Gislén, A., Dacke, M., Kröger, R.H.H., Abrahamsson, M., Nilsson, D.-E. and Warrant, E.J. (2003). Superior Underwater Vision in a Human Population of Sea Gypsies. *Current Biology*, [online] 13(10), pp.833–836. doi:https://doi.org/10.1016/S0960-9822(03)00290-2.

4. Hebb, D.O. (1949). *The organization of behavior: a neuropsychological theory.* Mahwah, N.J.: Erlbaum Ass.

5. Morell, P. and Quarles, R.H. (2017). *The Myelin Sheath.* [online] Nih.gov. Available at: https://www.ncbi.nlm.nih.gov/books/NBK27954/.

6. Lacourse, M.G., Orr, E.R. and Turner, J.A. (2003). Functional Cerebellar Activation During Novel And Learned Executed And Imagined Sequential Hand Movements. *Medicine & Science in Sports & Exercise*, 35(Supplement 1), p.S280. doi:https://doi. org/10.1097/00005768-200305001-01556.

7. Cleveland Clinic. (2021). *The Science is Clear: Why Multitasking Doesn't Work.* [online] Available at: https://health.clevelandclinic.org/ science-clear-multitasking-doesnt-work.

8. American Psychological Association (2006) *Multitasking: Switching costs, Apa.org.* Available at: https://www.apa.org/ topics/research/multitasking.

9. Watson, J.M. and Strayer, D.L. (2010). Supertaskers: Profiles in extraordinary multitasking ability. *Psychonomic Bulletin & Review*, [online] 17(4), pp.479–485. doi:https://doi. org/10.3758/PBR.17.4.479.

10. *The Impact of Interruptions | People & Culture* (no date) *hr.berkeley.edu.* Available at: https://hr.berkeley.edu/ impact-interruptions.

11. Russell, E.R. et al. (2019) 'Football's InfluencE on Lifelong health and Dementia risk (FIELD): protocol for a retrospective cohort study of former professional footballers', BMJ Open, 9(5), p. e028654. Available at: https://doi.org/10.1136/bmjopen-2018-028654.

12. Brené Brown. (n.d.). *Atlas of the Heart | Boundaries are a prerequisite for compassion and empathy.* [online] Available at: https://brenebrown.com/art/atlas-of-the-heart-boundaries-are-a-prerequisite-for-compassion-and-empathy/.

13. Worley, S.L. (2018). The Extraordinary Importance of Sleep: The Detrimental Effects of Inadequate Sleep on Health and Public Safety Drive an Explosion of Sleep Research. *PubMed*, 43(12), pp.758–763.

14. Bryant, E. (2021). *Lack of sleep in middle age may increase dementia risk.* [online] National Institutes of Health (NIH). Available at: https://www.nih.gov/news-events/nih-research-matters/lack-sleep-middle-age-may-increase-dementia-risk.

15. Tossell, K. *et al.* (2023) 'Somatostatin neurons in prefrontal cortex initiate sleep-preparatory behavior and sleep via the preoptic and lateral hypothalamus', *Nature Neuroscience*, pp. 1–15. Available at: https://doi.org/10.1038/s41593-023-01430-4.

16. Mead, M.N. (2008). Benefits of Sunlight: A Bright Spot for Human Health. *Environmental Health Perspectives*, [online] 116(4). doi:https://doi.org/10.1289/ehp.116-a160.

17. Kuzawa, C., & Blair, C. (2019). A hypothesis linking the energy demand of the brain to obesity risk. Proceedings of the National Academy of Sciences, 116(26), 13006-13011.

18. Muscaritoli, M. (2021) 'The Impact of Nutrients on Mental Health and Well-Being: Insights From the Literature', *Frontiers in Nutrition*, 8. Available at: https://doi.org/10.3389/fnut.2021.656290.

19. Rassovsky, Y. and Alfassi, T. (2019) 'Attention Improves During Physical Exercise in Individuals With ADHD', *Frontiers in Psychology*, 9(1). Available at: https://doi.org/10.3389/fpsyg.2018.02747.

20. Roig, M., Nordbrandt, S., Geertsen, S.S. and Nielsen, J.B. (2013). The effects of cardiovascular exercise on human memory: A review with meta-analysis. *Neuroscience & Biobehavioral Reviews*, 37(8), pp.1645–1666. doi:https://doi.org/10.1016/j.neubiorev.2013.06.012.

21. Aliyari, H., Golabi, S., Sahraei, H., Daliri, M.R., Minaei-Bidgoli, B., Tadayyoni, H. and Kazemi, M. (2022). Evaluation of Stress and Cognition Indicators in a Puzzle Game: Neuropsychological, Biochemical and Electrophysiological Approaches. [online] 77(4), pp.1397–1403. doi:https://doi.org/10.22092/ari.2021.356500.1855.

22. Gorvett, Z. (2019). *The tiny breaks that ease your body and reboot your brain.* [online] www.bbc.com. Available at: https://www.bbc.com/worklife/article/20190312-the-tiny-breaks-that-ease-your-body-and-reboot-your-brain.

23. synap.ac. (n.d.). *Synap - Online Exam & Assessment Platform.* [online] Available at: https://synap.ac/blog/top-10-surprising-memory-facts/.

24. Guan, A., Wang, S., Huang, A., Qiu, C., Li, Y., Li, X., Wang, J., Wang, Q. and Deng, B. (2022). The role of gamma oscillations in central nervous system diseases: Mechanism and treatment. *Frontiers in Cellular Neuroscience*, 16. doi:https://doi.org/10.3389/fncel.2022.962957.

25. Wnuk, A. (2018). *When the Brain Starts Adulting.* [online] Brainfacts.org. Available at: https://www.brainfacts. org/thinking-sensing-and-behaving/aging/2018/ when-the-brain-starts-adulting-112018.

26. Tooley, U.A., Bassett, D.S. and Mackey, A.P. (2021). Environmental influences on the pace of brain development. *Nature Reviews Neuroscience,* [online] 22(6), pp.372–384. doi:https://doi.org/10.1038/ s41583-021-00457-5.

27. Boyd, R. (2008). *Do People Only Use 10 Percent of Their Brains?* [online] Scientific American. Available at: https://www.scientificamerican.com/article/ do-people-only-use-10-percent-of-their-brains/.

28. BrainLine. (2012). *Can the Brain Itself Feel Pain?* [online] Available at: https://www.brainline.org/author/ brian-greenwald/qa/can-brain-itself-feel-pain.

29. ScienceDaily. (n.d.). *Understanding the speed of brain communication.* [online] Available at: https://www.sciencedaily. com/releases/2023/05/230511164625.htm [Accessed 17 Mar. 2024].

30. Padamsey, Z. and Rochefort, N.L. (2023) 'Paying the brain's energy bill', *Current Opinion in Neurobiology,* 78, p. 102668. Available at: https://doi.org/10.1016/j. conb.2022.102668.

31. Lim, S. *et al.* (2013) 'Preferential Detachment During Human Brain Development: Age- and Sex-Specific Structural Connectivity in Diffusion Tensor Imaging (DTI) Data',

Cerebral Cortex, 25(6), pp. 1477–1489. Available at: https://doi.org/10.1093/cercor/bht333.

Chapter Three: Mind

1. Rosenkranz, T., Takano, K., Watkins, E.R. and Ehring, T. (2020). Assessing repetitive negative thinking in daily life: Development of an ecological momentary assessment paradigm. *PLOS ONE*, 15(4), p.e0231783. doi:https://doi.org/10.1371/journal.pone.0231783.

2. Benedetti, F., Maggi, G., Lopiano, L., Lanotte, M., Rainero, I., Vighetti, S. and Pollo, A. (2003). Open versus hidden medical treatments: The patient's knowledge about a therapy affects the therapy outcome. *Prevention & Treatment*, 6(1). doi:https://doi.org/10.1037/1522-3736.6.1.61a.

3. Crum, A. J., & Langer, E. J. (2007). Mind-Set Matters: Exercise and the Placebo Effect. Psychological Science, 18(2), 165-171. https://doi.org/10.1111/j.1467-9280.2007.01867.x

4. Crum, A.J., Corbin, W.R., Brownell, K.D. and Salovey, P. (2011). Mind over milkshakes: Mindsets, not just nutrients, determine ghrelin response. *Health Psychology*, 30(4), pp.424–429. doi:https://doi.org/10.1037/a0023467.

5. Kahneman, D. (2011). *Thinking, Fast and Slow*. New York: Farrar, Straus and Giroux.

6. Csikszentmihalyi, M. (1990). *Flow: The Psychology of Optimal Experience*. New York: Harper and Row.

7. Engeser, Stefan. (2014). *Fluctuation of Flow and Affect in Everyday Life: A Second Look at the Paradox of Work.* Journal of Happiness Studies. 10.1007/s10902-014-9586-4.

8. UPI (1983). Study Ties I.Q. Scores To Stress. *The New York Times.* [online] 31 May. Available at: https://www.nytimes.com/1983/05/31/science/study-ties-iq-scores-to-stress.html.

9. Amen, D.G. (2016). *Change your brain, change your life.* London Piatkus (www.amenclinics.com).

10. Schwartz, J. and Gladding, R. (2012). *You are not your brain: the 4-step solution for changing bad habits, ending unhealthy thinking, and taking control of your life.* New York: Avery.

11. Katie, B. and Mitchell, S. (2017). *A mind at home with itself : how asking four questions can free your mind, open your heart, and turn your world around.* New York, New York: Harperone.

12. Josa, C. (2020). *Ditching Imposter Syndrome: how to finally feel good enough and become the leader you were born to be.* Hartfield: Beyond Alchemy Publishing.

13. Emmons, R. A., & McCullough, M. E. (2003). Counting blessings versus burdens: An experimental investigation of gratitude and subjective well-being in daily life. *Journal of Personality and Social Psychology,* 84(2), 377–389. https://doi.org/10.1037/0022-3514.84.2.377

14. The University of North Carolina at Chapel Hill. (n.d.). *Well Said: How Gratitude Affects Your Body and Brain.* [online]

Available at: https://www.unc.edu/discover/well-said-how-gratitude-affects-your-body-and-brain/ [Accessed 17 Mar. 2024].

15. Wilson, T.D., Reinhard, D.A., Westgate, E.C., Gilbert, D.T., Ellerbeck, N., Hahn, C., Brown, C.L. and Shaked, A. (2014). Just think: The challenges of the disengaged mind. *Science*, [online] 345(6192), pp.75–77. doi:https://doi.org/10.1126/science.1250830.

16. Pennebaker, J.W. (2017). Expressive Writing in Psychological Science. *Perspectives on Psychological Science*, 13(2), pp.226–229. doi:https://doi.org/10.1177/1745691617707315.

17. Netz, Y. (2017). Is the comparison between exercise and pharmacologic treatment of depression in the clinical practice guideline of the American College of Physicians evidence-based? *Frontiers in Pharmacology, 8*, 257.

18. Villani, D., Pancini, E., Pesce, F. and Scuzzarella, L. (2023). Savoring life during pandemic: an online intervention to promote well-being in emerging adults. *BMC Psychology*, 11(1). doi:https://doi.org/10.1186/s40359-023-01225-z.

Chapter Four: Body

1. Church, D. and Dispenza, J. (2019). *Mind to matter: the astonishing science of how your brain creates material reality.* Carlsbad, California: Hay House, Inc.

2. Porges, S.W. (2004). Neuroception: A subconscious system for detecting threats and safety. Zero to Three (j), 24(5), pp.19-24.

3. Porges, S.W. (2007). The polyvagal perspective. *Biological Psychology*, 74(2), pp.116–143. doi:https://doi.org/10.1016/j.biopsycho.2006.06.009.

4. Brown, R.P. and Gerbarg, P.L. (2005). Sudarshan Kriya Yogic Breathing in the Treatment of Stress, Anxiety, and Depression: Part II—Clinical Applications and Guidelines. *The Journal of Alternative and Complementary Medicine*, 11(4), pp.711–717. doi:https://doi.org/10.1089/acm.2005.11.711.

5. ScienceDaily. (n.d.). *How breathing shapes our brain.* [online] Available at: https://www.sciencedaily.com/releases/2022/11/221108120500.htm.

6. Golden, T.L., Tetreault, L., Ray, C.E., Kuge, M.N., Tiedemann, A. and Magsamen, S. (2021). The State of Music-Based Interventions for Mental Illness: Thought Leaders on Barriers, Opportunities, and the Value of Interdisciplinarity. *Community Mental Health Journal.* doi:https://doi.org/10.1007/s10597-021-00843-4.

7. Jacobson, E. (1974). *Progressive relaxation; a physiological and clinical investigation of muscular states and their significance in psychology and medical practice.* Chicago [Ill.] University Of Chicago Press.

8. www.va.gov. (n.d.). *Progressive Muscle Relaxation - Whole Health Library.* [online] Available at: https://www.va.gov/WHOLEHEALTHLIBRARY/tools/progressive-muscle-relaxation.asp.

Chapter Five: Stress Management

1. McEwen, B.S. and Stellar, E. (1993). Stress and the individual. Mechanisms leading to disease. *Archives of Internal Medicine*, [online] 153(18), pp.2093–2101. Available at: https://pubmed.ncbi.nlm.nih.gov/8379800/.

2. Peachy Essay. (2021). *Summary of Kelly McGonigal Ted Talk; How to make stress your friend.* [online] Available at: https://peachyessay.com/sample-essay/kelly-mcgonigal-ted-talk-stress-your-friend/.

3. Davidson, R.J., Kabat-Zinn, J., Schumacher, J., Rosenkranz, M., Muller, D., Santorelli, S.F., Urbanowski, F., Harrington, A., Bonus, K. and Sheridan, J.F. (2003). Alterations in Brain and Immune Function Produced by Mindfulness Meditation. *Psychosomatic Medicine*, 65(4), pp.564–570. doi:https://doi.org/10.1097/01.psy.0000077505.67574.e3.

4. Torre, J.B. and Lieberman, M.D. (2018). Putting Feelings Into Words: Affect Labeling as Implicit Emotion Regulation. *Emotion Review*, 10(2), pp.116–124. doi:https://doi.org/10.1177/1754073917742706.

5. Moser, J.S., Dougherty, A., Mattson, W.I., Katz, B., Moran, T.P., Guevarra, D., Shablack, H., Ayduk, O., Jonides, J., Berman, M.G. and Kross, E. (2017). Third-person self-talk facilitates emotion regulation without engaging cognitive control: Converging evidence from ERP and fMRI. *Scientific Reports*, 7(1). doi:https://doi.org/10.1038/s41598-017-04047-3.

6. *Home* (2024) *NeuroCapability*. Available at: https://neurocapability.com.au

7. Gollwitzer, P.M. and Sheeran, P. (2006). Implementation Intentions and Goal Achievement: A Meta-analysis of Effects and Processes. *Advances in Experimental Social Psychology*, [online] 38(1), pp.69–119. doi:https://doi.org/10.1016/s0065-2601(06)38002-1.

Chapter Six: Social Connection

1. Blum, K. (2012). Neuropsychiatric Genetics of Happiness, Friendships, and Politics: Hypothesizing Homophily ('Birds of a Feather Flock Together') as a Function of Reward

2. Penagos-Corzo, J.C., Cosio van-Hasselt, M., Escobar, D., Vázquez-Roque, R.A. and Flores, G. (2022). Mirror neurons and empathy-related regions in psychopathy: Systematic review, meta-analysis, and a working model. *Social Neuroscience*, 17(5), pp.462–479. doi:https://doi.org/10.1080/17470919.2022.2128868.

3. Woolfolk, A. (2020). *EDUCATIONAL PSYCHOLOGY: active learning edition, global edition*. S.L.: Pearson Education Limited.

4. Eysenck, M.W. and Keane, M.T. (2015). *Cognitive Psychology: a student's Handbook*. 7th ed. Abingdon, Oxon: Psychology Press.

5. Robert Waldinger (2016). *What makes a good life? Lessons from the longest study on happiness | Robert Waldinger. YouTube*. Available at: https://www.youtube.com/watch?v=8KkKuTCFvzI.

6. Hackett, R.A., Hudson, J.L. and Chilcot, J. (2020). Loneliness and type 2 diabetes incidence: findings from the English Longitudinal Study of Ageing. *Diabetologia*, 63(11), pp.2329–2338. doi:https://doi.org/10.1007/s00125-020-05258-6.

7. Stijovic, A., Forbes, P.A.G., Tomova, L., Skoluda, N., Feneberg, A.C., Piperno, G., Pronizius, E., Nater, U.M., Lamm, C. and Silani, G. (2023). Homeostatic Regulation of Energetic Arousal During Acute Social Isolation: Evidence From the Lab and the Field. *Psychological Science*, p.095679762311564. doi:https://doi.org/10.1177/09567976231156413.

8. Sethi, Y., Murli, H., Kaiwan, O., Vora, V., Agarwal, P., Chopra, H., Padda, I., Kanithi, M., Popoviciu, M.S. and Cavalu, S. (2022). Broken Heart Syndrome: Evolving Molecular Mechanisms and Principles of Management. *Journal of Clinical Medicine*, 12(1), p.125. doi:https://doi.org/10.3390/jcm12010125.

9. www.youtube.com. (n.d.). *The Power & Science of Social Connection: Emma Seppälä TEDx*. [online] Available at: https://www.youtube.com/watch?v=WZvUppaDfNs.

10. García-CampayoJ., Barceló-Soler, A., Martínez-Rubio, D., Navarrete, J., Adrián Pérez-Aranda, Feliu-Soler, A., Luciano, J.V., Baer, R.A., Willem Kuyken and Jesús Montero-Marín (2023). Exploring the Relationship Between Self-Compassion and Compassion for Others: The Role of Psychological Distress and Wellbeing. *Assessment*. doi:https://doi.org/10.1177/10731911231203966.

11. Warneken, F. and Tomasello, M. (2006). Altruistic Helping in Human Infants and Young Chimpanzees. *Science*, 311(5765), pp.1301–1303. doi:https://doi.org/10.1126/science.1121448.

12. Miller, D. T. (1999). The norm of self-interest. *American Psychologist*, 54(12), 1053–1060. https://doi.org/10.1037/0003-066X.54.12.1053

13. Nichol, B., Wilson, R., Rodrigues, A. and Haighton, C. (2023). Exploring the Effects of Volunteering on the Social, Mental, and Physical Health and Well-being of Volunteers: An Umbrella Review. *VOLUNTAS: International Journal of Voluntary and Nonprofit Organizations*. doi:https://doi.org/10.1007/s11266-023-00573-z.

14. Melamend, David et al. The Robustness of Reciprocity: Experimental Evidence That Each Form of Reciprocity Is Robust to the Presence of Other Forms of Reciprocity." *Science Advances*, vol. 6, no. 23, June 2020, p. eaba0504, https://doi.org/10.1126/sciadv.aba0504. Accessed 11 July 2020

15. Gilbert, D. (2009). *Stumbling on Happiness*. HarperCollins UK.

16. ResearchGate. (n.d.). *(PDF) Lottery Winners and Accident Victims: Is Happiness Relative?* [online] Available at: https://www.researchgate.net/publication/22451114_Lottery_Winners_and_Accident_Victims_Is_Happiness_Relative.

17. Lyubomirsky, S. (2007). *The How of Happiness: A practical guide to getting the life you want*. Penguin Press.

.

Acknowledgments

There are so many people to thank for supporting me on the journey that has led to the birth of this book, right back from when I was young and my wonderful father instilled in me the importance of being true to who I am. I grew up in a very male-dominated environment, a working farm, and the fact that I was female counted for nothing. Everything the men could do, I was expected to do. There were no allowances made. Nothing was beyond me because I happened to be female. The word "can't" did not exist, and any whining or excuses due to my sex were given short shrift.

I did not realise until I left that environment how rare and special it was. It was only when I entered the more corporate world that suddenly being female was a point of difference. It was somewhat of a shock at the time, and it would have been easy to succumb to the prevailing view and associated stereotypes. My father sadly passed away when I was 26 years old, but his philosophy and the confidence and independence he instilled in me has carried me through the best and the worst of times. To him, I will always be grateful – he sowed the seeds of the person I became.

Through the ebbs and flows of my life, I have met so many wonderful people who have shaped, taught, and changed me.

Special thanks must go to all the coaches and guides who have helped me on my way such as Dr Kim Jobst, Marina Dieck, Lesley McBride, Karen Evans, Jennie Flower, and Catherine May. All of whom have become dear friends as time has passed.

Thanks to my fabulous sister-in-law, Beverley Dobson, my wonderful brother Antony and their family, and my equally wonderful Auntie Sandra and Uncle John Slater, whom I could not have survived without; plus my long-time friends, Teresa Threadgold, Jo Simmons, and Sue Chipchase, who have wiped away my tears when needed and held me tight when we collapsed in laughter.

A very special thanks goes to my three children, now all grown and independent in their own right, Jack, Harry and Katie: I am so proud of you all. You have been by my side for the best part of my life. You have looked after me, cared for me, and loved me in a way a mother can only dream of. I consider myself to be truly blessed to have you as my family. Even better, we now have Rosie and Alice who have joined our tribe; I could not ask for two more perfect daughters-in-law and, of course, our amazing bundle of joy, my grandson, Finn. And so, our family continues to grow and expand with more joy every day. It has not been easy and sometimes quite tough, but we have always been there for each other. We hold each other tight, and for that, I am the most grateful person in the world.

Big thanks must also go to all those who have made this book possible, particularly Emily Gowor, who held my hand and provided encouragement every step of the way; Ursula

McCabe who did a wonderful job of the edit process, and all those involved in the birth of this book. Many thanks go to you all. I must also not forget all those I have worked with over the past 25+ years, within the agencies, the consultancies, the coaching community, and all the businesses I have had the privilege to partner with as clients. It has been without doubt a wonderfully fulfilling journey with so many of you contributing so much to my life and my ongoing learning. I would not be here without you, and I owe you all so much. You know who you are. Thank you.

Finally, there is one very special person I must thank before signing off, and that is my husband, Giuseppe Donvito. You have been my soulmate for the past 17 years now. You have supported me, guided me, shaped me, and loved me in a way I've never experienced before. You fill me up every single day. You cherish the essence of me, the good, the bad, and the ugly. Without you, I would not be here today, happy, smiling, and full of love. I was somewhat broken when you found me. You healed me and helped me find the way to being whole again. Thank you.

Deborah